EVE ESCAPES

EVE ESCAPES
Ruins and Life

HÉLÈNE CIXOUS

TRANSLATED BY PEGGY KAMUF

polity

First published in French as *Ève s'évade* © Éditions Galilée, 2009

This English edition © Polity Press, 2012

Ouvrage publié avec le concours du Ministère français de la Culture –
Centre national du livre

Published with the assistance of the French Ministry of Culture – National
Centre for the Book

Polity Press
65 Bridge Street
Cambridge CB2 1UR, UK

Polity Press
350 Main Street
Malden, MA 02148, USA

ISBN-13: 978-0-7456-5096-8
ISBN-13: 978-0-7456-5097-5 (pb)

A catalogue record for this book is available from the British Library.

Typeset in 10.75 on 14 pt Janson Text
by Servis Filmsetting Ltd, Stockport, Cheshire
Printed and bound in Great Britain by the MPG Books Group

For further information on Polity, visit our website: www.politybooks.com

CONTENTS

Day of Sufferance   1

The Prisoner's Dream   17

Freud Dreams No More   45

The Shrinking   61

Tales and Days of Reading   81

The Cane and the Parasol   95

On Board the Magnolia   123

I Become a Cemetery Citizen   145

Translator's Notes   163

DAY OF SUFFERANCE

It is thus the New Life which I see. Its aged face where eternal youth shines. Right in front of me and caught up in a rush. I saw that I was seeing time fall

This emotion

Sitting in front of Mama who was no longer Mama but Omi herself – I was struck by distance I saw Omi who was Mama as if through a thickening of my crystalline lens, enlarged by the presence of a perceptible distance between us, a distance of so much time, and this time was, I guessed, the one that was looming, the one that was going to come, the one that would come, a folio of imminent things – I was not seeing Mama, I was making her out, I was holding her, despite myself, at the end of this invisible spyglass that the filter of foreboding inserts between us when we are hurried motionless into the fated future. I saw her masked with distance, she was smiling very broadly at me, the prominence of her teeth brushed with a strange sparkle of love held my gaze, they were like the double of her teeth, which she held out to me tenderly, my heart groaned, my inner dog, he lay flat and groaned although Mama did not hear my soul sounds

From this distance I made out Mama's pupils, which were laughing, laughing, skipping about in mischief, the trick they were playing on me, "I am an old woman who is still human," she said, that was Mama, and that laugh was not Omi, but just when I was about to believe it, she turned terribly pale, and that white on the lips was Omi – "wait!" she said, shaken by a little anxiety, guessing that I was going to retire upstairs to my writing study, and this, this was new for Mama, this little call frightened by not knowing what she was afraid of, what she wanted, "wait!" and what was she looking for, what did she want to remember, this had never been Mama, this frail fear, and not Omi either, "do you want something, little Mama?" and this, these words in that voice, that had never been me, in a deep shiver I *saw* us, we were trembling old veal calves who, having been moved at night, through incalculable darkness, from an habitual lodging, wake up in the unknown daylight of another world. The day before will never come again. Never again will we climb at a lively pace the marble steps of the life before.

I forbade it, this immense pain. I retained only the feeling of immensity that this prodigious piece of an hour had given me.

"I want a second slice of toast," said omified Mama. That had never been Mama. This was the first time. She had found what she wanted to want. The slice of toast was the plank over the abyss. Solid, probable, reassuring. "I want-a-second-slice-of toast!" had procured for Omi-Mama the satisfaction one feels when slotting in the missing piece. That was Omi all right. She always loved little triumphs. Never, Mama would never have, had, has never been able to ask anyone in the world, never been able to ask for what she's always done by herself for herself. Having always been for herself her whole household, her mistress and her servant, herself herselves. This was therefore no longer Mama. "She has changed places" was the thought thrown at me.

So *without any delay*, at least perceivable, at the speed of lightning-thought,

I hurled myself with a leap into Mama's old age. Pray, I thought, while leaping and in the very time of the leap, that Mama not feel, not have had the time to notice the least trace of the threat of anachronism between us. If there was a delay, I filled it in. I went to the kitchen to get a second slice of toast for Mama sitting in the dining room in front of her cup of café au lait *exactly* as if thousands of times I had made this trip that I had never made. I invented a habit in mid-air.

"Mama is being replaced," a thought briefly thought, and I acted quickly as if it was not I who was thinking and who was replacing Mama. Furtive thoughts in the dark corners of my dome, they thrash against the ceiling so silently that I doubt they really nest up high to the right, they are perhaps but the illusory wings of the Fears. The Fears, here is a species of Chiroptera that escapes all scientific observation. When their slight, imponderable and mute phantoms brush against our hair, we never know if they are real or figures beneath the forehead, if they are in the present or if they scurry along in that other time which we dread absolutely because it will happen to us and it will happen to us only as the Forbidden itself. It will get to us and we will not get there. It is what awaits us so as to nail us to our own bones.

I let the thought get lost over the stove. These thoughts have the briefest life. They are extinguished at the speed of forgetting a dream.

I returned in a second with the desired slice of toast, and Mama carefully spread cream on the outline. The passion for cream, that's Omi.

These accelerations galvanize my brain. My brain and I are living in a new apartment, much larger and more bizarrely conceived than the former one. To see myself with Omi for Mama is to have the cane of old age for being.

I noted down all this with great difficulty and retouching, limping the words, with anxious and awkward gropings, reading with the tips of my eyelashes the vision called Premonition, which occupied the whole expanse of the canvas, I was filled with tears all down my throat –

I noted down all this, I noted, in one of those large Leader Price notebooks that Mama used to buy for me in the past – I start again: that she doesn't buy for me anymore, that she stopped buying for me, going to buy for me, because she has stopped going to the market, her perimeter of movement has shrunk, she has stopped going into the garden alone and under her own steam, while I began to try to paint the radiant vision of Mama (seized mutated transfixed turned translated) into Omi, of Mama omified, I had reached out my right arm toward the pile of notebooks and copybooks and pulled from the pile at random one of those large letter pads best price *meilleur prix mejor precio* that were for years the canvas signed spirit-of-Mama on which I have painted so much. This notebook, I saw, contained a first page dated July 12, 2003, which is an uncertain indication because all the dates dotting my texts are half-fictions, imprecisions kept secret, even from me. This notebook thus added a floating time to the set of times that were crowding – a people of cherished and anxious traces – all around the edges of the True Vision.

I saw that I was seeing the Truth. I was seeing true. I kept its silence. Yet I had almost a need to break it, an audacious need, temerarious but timid, a timirarious need, one of those movements of the soul that are ready to take flight when they step forward. So I said: "Things going OK, Mama?"

And more precisely: "Are things going OK, Mama?" Thus I urged her on a little. I cracked open the door for Truth. She was omified, but all the same Mama. She could tell me everything a little. I was well aware that everything happening to us was very difficult to say, to think, to think to say, no one is sure of anything, no one stands on anything, sitting a little on the other's side, there is amphibology everywhere, in the articulations, in the interior monologues, and for a good reason, this kind of alteration, both clear-cut and fluctuating, overcomes all the characters, from the moment Mama was Omi too me too, I contracted a slight stuttering of thought, I was speaking to Mama, but I clearly felt that one of the intonations of my voice, a certain flexibility, came from the voice that in the past, a long time ago, I used to address to Omi. I even recognized, in a manner of leaning forward and pushing out my words, a few at a time, and like mouthfuls of bread, toward her eyes, the kind of gentleness that in the past I used to send toward Omi, in consideration of her age, of her very small size, of how the different exiles had made her force fragile, and it all made me unhappy. To be gentle with Mama struck me with sadness.

Pray that I have the strength of conscience needed to note down these signs of time lag, these processes of contamination, at a moment when the gust of an emotion virtually threw me to the ground beside my chair, at Mama's feet, this shows just how much the shock of the apparition had split me apart, disjointed me, and how much I was a stranger to myself, by the blow of Mama's Omification. The question arose in me: did Mama have, by way of reflections, a retouched Vision of "me"? Did she see, in my different aspects, that I saw in her something that she did not see or that she perhaps hid from herself and that worried me? When I say "Things going OK, Mama?" it is a serious, intense question, I mean: "where are things going, Mama? Do you know?" I set it down for an

5

instant on the table, before her cup of café au lait, then "on the telephone," that is to say, on that invisible telephone with which one goes deeper, from thought to thought, in this way perhaps she will be able to tell me the things she puts carefully aside, behind a corner of thought straight as a gate, so as to avoid losing them altogether, and so as at the same time not to be able to find them again. The things that are in her head and that she does not recognize and that preoccupy her like a raw silk blouse which she has been wearing lately with a certain surprise because every day she wonders where it came from. Prey to the feeling Freud described, under the name of screen-impression of the never seen. The mystery of the blouse occupies all her reflections. If she could resolve it, it seems to her that All she hides from herself would be revealed to her. The raw silk looks like the piece of green fabric stretched over a window pane that had been broken in the window of the pantry, so as to bog down the attention of the narrator who meant to cross the room in search of past time, believing he was in the salon when in fact he was on the other side. Where does it come from? she wonders every two or three hours. The silk resists. My mother as well. Where are we going? I ask myself.

Perhaps, I thought, she will be able to say a key-sentence to me on the heels of "I am an old woman who is still human," which would allow me perhaps to get a clear and immediate idea as to the station where she's waiting for me, which is now inaccessible to me. She is perhaps ahead of me. Perhaps she has been on the way to Omification for a long time and was humbly and patiently waiting for me to join her? For me to recognize her?

– Yes, things are going OK mydaughter, and you, did you sleep OK? Her wisp of a voice crackles, stumbles, almost breaks and with a vibrating effort hoists itself up to -K.

I am losing time.

It is an awful loss that I myself am making, while making every effort.

– Where are we going? I say. – To London, says the dream. Get ready. The dream discovers my new apartment, while I am readying my baggage. It is a beautiful morning. The dream is pregnant. When I see its belly, I rectify: it is, then, a feminine Dream. Above all don't miss the train. The Dream is lively, active, and beneath her round, warm eyes Mama's smile is attached. She finds the apartment much bigger than the other. Myself, I think it is interesting, pleasant, light, without any ulterior motive. One can hear a chorus of school children. No doubt there is a school very close by. When approaching the bay window you look out on a narrow, flower-lined path peopled with a line of schoolchildren, who are buzzing as in the present days and like the buzzing of my mother when she inspects the row of geraniums, her arm knotted in my arm. I am a little distracted, getting lost in thought associations I follow a comparison, I get lost, the Dream is ready. One must have breakfast. One must be in London by 10 o'clock, no later. Nine o'clock at the airport station. It will soon be 8 o'clock. I still have an hour. The hours buzz. London rings. – London? you say. What is London? She doesn't answer. I shake London, *Londres, l'onde, l'ombre, long, londi, allons dre.* Come on hurry up, the Dream is in front of you. I gather up my things, which gives you an idea of the Dispersion, it's like gathering up dispersion, there is some everywhere to be forgotten and then I am traversed by the bald blade of a Fear. The Fear of Forgetting flutters in front of me, and naturally I forget the urgency of gathering things. If I could put my suitcase on the couch, what would I be putting on the couch? According to Wilhelm Stekel the baggage you take with you is the weight of the sins by which you feel crushed. I hesitate.

My sins escape me. Oh! Toiletries. And the word *toilette*, how long it has been apostrophizing me. A first-rate mocker. You, *toi*, who is always missing a letter, like the tooth missing from the woman singer who allurepels Stendhal. But, I say, it's Mama who gave me this suitcase. I love it. I could take the suitcase, the suitcase itself, that will suffice for my needs. Moreover according to Freud it is often precisely the case that baggage symbolizes without a doubt our own genital organs. According to me the suitcase is the uterus of the dream. The Dream has her suitcase in front, my mother travels with her pack on her back. On my side, I am never separated from my suitcase full of unique notebooks. The value of my suitcase increases with time. Its powers never cease growing, in reality, symbolically, in French and in memories. It can do almost anything. And with charm and discretion. It is light brown. Here is its new function: starting this year it has taken on the role of Tomb

Finally I do it: put the suitcase on the couch. Each word, each gesture, counts. I open it. It is open. An idea occurs to me: perhaps the totally incomprehensible and paradoxical pleasure, which consequently is unaccepted by me and many times shoved with my foot back under the couch all year long, which entered like a wedge into my mental space, a psychical curiosity that I have spoken about to no one, characterized rather by the absence of repulsion, horror, rejection, where one might normally expect to find them, and by the undeniable presence of a feeling of well-being where everyone else would feel fear, perhaps this kind of tolerable happiness, which I had never heard anyone speak of, and which arose in the spring when I had acquired the tomb, perhaps this foreign body that has grown in my head, which should kill me and does not prevent me from living, this burial chamber in the brain with which, to my great surprise, I am quite at home, would find an explanation in the suitcase: either that I am remaking the suitcase for myself with the tomb. Or that the suitcase has always lived by my side as a portable tomb, a chest of secrets, an earth-colored animal. This idea and the ones following came out of the suitcase as soon as I pulled on the zipper. I am losing time. But I would be unintelligible if I didn't note down here a few dates and facts. I follow the order of the accidents. Thus, in 2005, but perhaps it was in 2006, it didn't really have a date because it was eternity breaking through, in Algiers, I found my father again, his tomb, being one on one with him, although it seemed to me that ten steps behind our embrace there was an improbable flute player, true or dream, this took place and I remember it, if we had not been alone, I say to myself, the prodigy could perhaps not have taken place.

In March 2007, at the end of a long series of chance events, for the most part unfortunate, and all of them necessary, I won't tell the story but I see it clearly, I obtained via official letter, against every expectation, the promise of some posses sion, uncertain, on my side, like a property that is unspeakable, unappropriable, undesirable, inestimable, address, location, passport window, place, room, ticket, vehicle, dock, port, entry, vessel, I don't know what, on the other side, according to the Law and the Office, a thing named "Concession" – a word designed to induce humility in those who are granted it – in the Cemetery, the *Cimetière*, called "Ci." This event, as is suddenly obvious to me when I open the suitcase, changed my whole life. I have only just received the notice, with the delay that frequently accompanies events that surpass us. The same day as the Concession, *Tombe* was republished, a book that I had omitted frequenting since 1972, date on which, although I have never realized this before these pages, all corporal link with my father within the tomb and as a tomb was interrupted forever, at least until the contrary reappari-tion, and without my being able to do anything about it.

There must be a hidden relation between these two events, but I don't see it. I see in my imagination these three unequal rectangular volumes. They look like letters sealed in destiny's envelope.

To come back to the suitcase on the couch – but I panic: my passport! I pat myself down. It is indeed in my right pocket, slender cardboard rectangle. I drink barely a sip of coffee, and it's the last minute.

We hurry. Here we are in the Train without Dream. She must have taken the car in front I say to myself, but we are in the same train, I reassure myself. I am alone with my brother, without a coat, without any woolens. I am going to be cold. I see us getting off at the airport. The baggage is unloaded onto a conveyor belt. Dream comes back toward me smiling the smile that my mother wears from now on. It's a look of ravishments, a hymn to life that death concedes to us. It means: "It is better to be old than dead." I read this sentence in my mother's thought. Dream has already finished with the formalities. She has passed through customs. I am still waiting for my suitcase. When I see it, the first one to arrive, I put my hand on it, it is not mine, it's a mistake. Some time passes in front of me. I walk along the baggage conveyor, but not one is my suitcase. The fear of a delay is preaching to me: how far away already is the time of dawn when I thought I was leaving for London in a little while. Suddenly the conveyor stops. In my head the sentence doesn't have time to write itself to the end. One can read: the conveyor sto. Nothing is moving anymore. I cast a last glance. Everything is stopped. I understood that it was a death. I had lost time.

– *Et toi mafille, tu as bien dor-mi*? My mother's voice hoists itself from syllable to syllable, squeaks on all the hoarse vowels up to the last syllable. Once at *-mi*, it rests. Pause. Sentence

10

accomplished. A modest satisfaction colors her cheeks. The world rises now before her everything is inclined at every moment it's necessary to carry the whole burden one's two arms are hardly enough with their hands spread wider and wider into fists with their thickened fingers to raise the trunk, the slopes, the long and rough ropes of the sentences weighed down with knots and many modalizing ornaments. She lives surrounded, followed, hedged in by staircases, there is one just in front of her bed, between her bedroom and the dining room, the chairs are so many steps in her way. She dreams in short of an ideal, pruned, rich but sober language, as light as the silkiest silk, like the one that we speak between the cats and me, but without cooing because for that you need a supple throat, without *i*'s and without *u*'s the *o*'s and *a*'s being flatter and thus more practical. Moreover she has already tried it out a few times. Soon she'll be able to say: *et toi mafille* (the *ma* helps her get out *fille*) *ta bien dorma*? That is what seems pleasant and worthwhile to her. Often this dreamed-of language even formulates practical models exactly by itself, without any effort on her part. Since she is not its author but its user, she casts a quick glance at my face (*visage* is avoided) to see if it passes muster. It does, Mama, I reassure her little visage, which is more and more mobile. She uses it as a supplement. I admire the number of utterances she can translate into shudders, shimmers, looks. Thus I say to myself we have been going to school for the last few months, it took me some time to realize it, we are acquiring new basic skills, Mama is writing otherwise and in that very moment I can see to read. Myself I have changed languages, but not fluently, I tinker together a speech especially for Mama, a little bit secret, clipped squared off, not at all ruminated, not equivocal, as if cut out of jute fabric, rough even, straightforward and totally asyndetic, on which she can get a sharp and firm hold.

And on the landing of *-mi*, Mama stands still in the state

11

of the god of the seventh day with a foot on the spade chin on the handle of the tool, and as if come back to herself, pulled out of the phase of Omification, she looks at me with delight while I look at her with delight on the one hand like a young mother looks at her baby who looks at her blissfully, the one nourishing the other with light, in such a way that from the two faces emanates the double radiance that is called beauty,

on the other hand – since this appears to me in the middle ground and thanks to a stretching out of time that delays its earths and its days in vast depths around our two characters held in suspension – she looks at me look at her looking at me looking at her with long warm sweetened reinvigorating draughts, drinking us up in a thick, sublime drinking, while resembling in a way that is fascinating for me, as if I was discovering in that moment that we were the unexpected and absolutely unquestionable double of the couple Cimon and Pero, linked by the supreme milk.

This is a fact. I cannot explain it. This scene takes place in front of the banister of thirty-foot-high iron rails that stand guard over the floors of the house and that Mama grasps in order to make the every day more difficult climb that takes her from her bedroom to the bathroom. The difference between the staircase in Montaigne's Tower and the staircase in my mother's tower is the high rails. At the end Montaigne no longer descended the steps that would have led him from his bedroom to the chapel, for lack of the black rails that serve Mama as prosthesis. He contents himself with making a few somewhat shaky steps hastened by that weakness of age that is pushing him from behind, sometimes using the wall to lean on, especially when there is no one to see him, sometimes even when there is someone, and in this way while tottering he reaches the divine port, cut into a notch in the auditive fireplace, sits down on the prayer stool, having given up kneeling since that familiar joy has been taken away from him by the rigors of nature. The steps that lead from the bedroom to the chapel and vice versa, no one except maybe angels ever took them.

Custodes hominum psalimus Angelos
naturae fragili quos Pater addidit
caelestis comites . . .

– What is that? says my mother. I hear singing? – Curlews, I say. – Curlews? – Water woodcocks, I say. They're screaming. Danger no doubt.

Insidiantibus/ne succumberet hostibus.

And indeed, my mother sways, her right foot caught in a piece of clothing, her left hand grabs the rail again, climbs.

My nurseling is old, thinks the Tower.

She is fitted out in the pink dressing gown that was Omi's long ago and saddled on her shoulders are the towels whose equipment is inseparable from this expedition. All around her, a high-wire act of the present summer days and the days she lived in past cities, in the pretty guises that were hers and in many colors, flutters at the bars. In this moment everything has a double that casts a luminous golden dust in my eyes. Although I recognize the interior colors in which dreams are painted, I myself am not at all in a dream. These optical phenomena occur in certain realities. I see in reality as many Eves crowding all smiles around Mama as Adriennes around the Sylvies who crowd hurriedly around Nerval when they flee upon leaving the Loisy ball into the thickets of blooming thorns dragging with them the garlands of time. It seems to me I have already seen more than once in many places that are nevertheless very distant from each other the cross-pieces that come to lean against the bars. The principal reality is indeed Mama, who is dated precisely by that insistent pink of the cheeks produced by the prolonged use of cortisone. My brother claims there is also a small oedema,

13

but I don't see it. All the other realities are a little unreal, but I see them, without harboring any illusions, nearby, glowing, as if lacquered with a fine dew produced by my own tears. However much I'd like to hold them back, they will not obey me. They are going to leave us, soon. But as long as this soon keeps us waiting, I enjoy everything about this close contact, this living album.

I lower my head. I cover Mama's face with measured kisses taking care not to wrinkle her skin, I place some on her ears, on the stems of her glasses, on her forehead, everywhere except on the nose. She accepts my caresses with the gentle consent of a sheep. I hum: "Mama dearest, my little sheep, my green beans, my magic kitten, my joy in the dungeon," a whole litany of which she understands nothing.

To be born I must return to my heart of hearts. That is the law. One obeys the law blindly. Blindness is the condition and the sign that one is on one's own fated path. The blindness can last eternally or –

When the day comes to be born I return to the Tower. That is the Law. I have to return to my point of departure. One cannot argue with it: I must return to my heart of hearts, that is my strength and it's stronger than I am, nothing except death could keep me from it. When the day comes I go to be born to the Tower. I go, I surrender myself. One obeys the law blindly. Neither defeat nor victory nor knowledge, one crawls to the natal nest. It is because I surrender that I crawl. It is by the fact that I see myself crawling and crossing with pain and anguish excruciating distances that I recognize the absolute Authority: I am called, and it is Life itself that is on the telephone. Life without Face, Call without Call. The Force to which one does not even say yes. There is no no that stirs in front of it. It breathes. As soon as it breathes it moves. It me's. I don't hear its words, there is no harangue or preaching, I understand nothing, the internal gust raises me up, my soul shudders, I do not flee, I do not argue, one cannot not. The soaring is. Then comes the path. Mine is long, arduous, mean. That is my lot. Others than myself have a different fate. I know a poet whose heart of hearts was in his neighborhood. Passy. Rue de la Pompe.

THE PRISONER'S DREAM

That the Tower's personality might be a double of my mother, will I have had then to approach the end for this to become apparent to me? I have been there a hundred times, for fifty years I have been overlooking the key. Every year I go there once with my brother, sometimes with my beloved, I have to leave early in the morning, leave my mother behind me, I am not thinking anything, there is a call and I'm the one who answers, automatically, I walk, to the Tower, to which I come to reignite writing, when I arrive at the Tower, I approach its body always from the same side, I stretch out my right hand, I touch with my fingers the point where writing lies, and right away it starts up again. This gesture is necessary, powerful and immutable. I have never begun any life without birth taking place according to the script I have just described, or book, or love, or rediscovery or survival, without this reaffirmed wedding without ceremonies but with an absolute exactitude.

But before the Tower there is my mother. On the way back I am thinking only of her.

It is very difficult to go to Montaigne.

One can arrive there only after delays, the first day of July at the moment of leaving the departure slips away beneath a storm, the number of turns of the screw varies, as does their interval. The third day my brother's car will break down on the highway, it will take fully a lost night and three mornings before we will find ourselves the fourth day on the sad and so fervently desired road, it is always Hell to go to Paradise and how many cruel deeds one has had to commit, this morning's little crime accompanies me in the car, one brings along in one's head a little girl with a face aggrieved by mute fears, it's my mother who whispers and to whom I do not listen, I bound away and let her get smaller along the roadside without turning around, I have never felt the double pang as I did this morning, I say this to myself every year, I cannot abandon my mother on the bank, I cannot not abandon her, the little matricide is a little infanticide, I have never felt so much the intoxicating scent of dawn edged by pines that is exhaled by the secret of my crime against humanity. – Go faster, I murmur. – Let me dawdle, replies my brother. The torture propagates. What I inflict on my mother is inflicted in turn on me. I can't say to my brother: I want to go back home to Mama since I am asking him to take me away from my mother who is my child.

She did not even whisper. It's her eyes that widened in my ear, without you what will become of me? I suddenly recognized the look of this distress: it was far way, in Oran, the world was broken, I was climbing on the edge of the cliff, a panicked anxiety grabbed hold of me, I wanted to put on my sandals but it wasn't working, they were not mine, I pleaded with Mama to come back to fetch me right away. I had lost sight of her. I looked for her, blind, I yelled out her name like someone gone mad. I knew very well that the strength of the cry would reach nowhere, but I cried as if it could, while sobbing in a heart-rending voice. I was not going to find her. I was alone. My anxiety was all the greater in that I was three years old. It was my whole future life that was happening to me in advance. Running brought me to a little café where a waitress reigned. I addressed the unknown woman tearfully. Where is the train? The station? The bus? It leaves in ten minutes, the waitress said to me in German. Do you have some money? Then she explained to me at length where the bus was, all of this in German. I thought I understood that I had to go out, turn right. I ran out. But outside I saw nothing. I saw an erasure. Outside was maybe outside, out of this outside? More outside? I so wished that the German waitress would guide me at least to the outside. I saw myself lost. I will never again return home. I wept. Now it's Mama who is searching with tears. The waitress speaks to her in German, but she doesn't hear. What use is seeing to her? She doesn't hear me.

By all appearances it's a trip to Montaigne. Years go by. I weave my cloth, I tear it, I repair it, the rip is still just as young. With age youth gets worse. Today is the first time I hear myself thinking: this time is perhaps the last. It is such a frightening thought that I cannot stay near it. I don't want it to find a present in reality. I hate it, more or less. Then I don't care a bit about it. It's not a prophecy, I say to myself. It's a comedy. It falls into the category of false premonitions with which one seeks to harm oneself. Let's not think about it anymore. One forgets it.

One thinks it's easy to get from A to M, but not at all. The road network resists like a spider web, the conducting circuits don't form a continuous spiral; on the contrary for a distance of a sixty miles the route blocked by the forces of worldwide lorries stops being smooth and straight and becomes a thread zigzagged with ornaments, with reverse turns back round on itself by the interior of the main road, over which the threat

19

of death looms, one drives between hazards. Finally we had the always renewed pleasure of being greeted by the goddess of Dordogne: the little Virgin in a blue mantle who is a prettily proportioned miniature woman, slender, perched on a tree, her wings folded, waited for us at the edge of the river. From here on everything calms down. The villages compete in elegance and faithfulness. They are still just as much in flower.

One recognizes the sky's reflections on the linden trees and the waters. One is getting closer. That's when one is stopped. Monstrous cranes produced by some demon's imagination block the road, face off at the crossroads that would have brought us to Saint Pey and from there to the Tower. There's no way to get through or back up. The male machines engage in hand-to-hand combat, rise up while sliding beneath their serrated abdomens enormous shoveling paws, and throw each other over, spill their stock of sperm on the pavement. So close to the goal, one has to give up. Once the blockage is finally lifted, one will go no farther night is falling, the Tower is put off until Tomorrow.

To come back to my mother, the idea occurs to me that I never do anything but come back to my mother, when I return to the Tower, I go from my mother to the Tower and as soon as I leave my mother behind I go as quickly as possible toward the Tower so as to come back to my mother with the tense urgency that stirs me while I am entirely focused on what I expect from the Tower, I believed, because I have deposited my memory and my powers for safekeeping there, I go from my mother to the Tower, but the idea has never occurred to me I that could not return from the Tower to my mother, in the same day, that is why we have to leave early in the morning, so as to come back to my mother before dark, thereupon as soon as I see the sayings inscribed on the beams of the Liberary by Montaigne, I see the sayings of my mother, my mother's different sorts of courage are exactly those of Montaigne, to the point that believing I go from my mother to the Tower it's as if I was going from my mother to a double of my mother, whose charms are powerfully enhanced by writing, to the point that the nostalgia I have for the Tower as soon as I am there turns into nostalgia for my mother, and I had never yet noticed this movement which is that of my very life, its secret clockworks, before this day in the year 2008.

I was standing next to the Tower when I saw, my brother being still inside, the Vision of what I had never seen

It is as if I had just awakened.

The apocalypse takes place at the very moment I am writing these lines. But it seems to me it must have begun to dawn like a supernatural day at the somewhat vague moment when, being in the Tower exactly as usual, with the same intense attention to my reverie and the same very powerful distraction in which I envelop the Mind so as to keep myself distant from the entourage, an image came to surprise me in my silent and calculated withdrawal, with enough force to draw me out of the absolute silence I maintain once I penetrate within these revered walls. Not being in fact able to fulfill my desire to be absolutely alone with my thoughts and those dear to me in the Tower, a privilege that reality excludes, my whole life I have escaped from others' company by slipping myself, as soon as the door opens that gives access to the deepest heart of hearts, into the box of a hermetic solitude. This withdrawal would never have been possible without the agreement and spontaneous complicity of my brother whom I have never had to ask to provide a diversion so that my solitude could hide behind his tall and wide silhouette, for on his own he fills the role of hospitality, being the one who talks without stopping while I am silent, he engages at length the young girls who serve as ushers and guides and in whom he discovers pretty features, a liveliness, a pleasant face, meanwhile charm does its work, and while the Tower bristles with old stories and little idylls, I totally surrender myself to my enchantments. What would I do, what have I done, at the Tower, internally, year after year? I would touch its walls with my fingers and its ceilings with my looks, I would invoke the powers of writing, I would bathe my soul in the rivers of unknown thoughts that genius unrolls when surrounded by the song of all the books its heart receives the marvelous measures of its own speech, I would relive Creation according to Montaigne, I would give myself up to one of those Delphic cults about which nothing is known and nothing must be said even to oneself because they are as insubstantial as hallucinations, but just as majestic and exhilarating, I would witness the real and supernatural events of the Life of Montaigne, I would manage easily to insert my thought into his reveries, and more than once I was there at the first appearance of a sentence which I observed as the larva then the mutation and the breathtaking unfolding of the sublime body that surges up as if by miracle from a dead shell, but it is not a miracle, it is a natural phenomenon. Sentences would stir in my chest: there was always fertilization. Toward noon I would begin to imagine my mother who was alone and far away. Her image would quickly grow, I would fling myself out of the Tower, urging my brother to leave the Tower behind us as soon as possible, to gulp down his sandwiches without delay, to come back to my mother, trembling endlessly at the perils of the road, threatened with dying before seeing my mother again, surrounded by the ghosts of road accidents whose sinister squadrons I could make out laying siege to Mama at the same moment, as if I were fleeing a punishment.

I come back to the time and the place of the Apocalypse: it is noon, I am alone with the Tower beside me, I have left my brother inside, in a lively conversation with the young usher who is reciting the discreet description of the temple.

That is when I see appear before me, above some tufts of bleeding hearts, the Vision that I recognize as destined for me since forever, and that for forty years had remained unnoticed, very close, and kept invisible for the whole duration of my blindness. And by the strange laws of the soul's optics, it is once I exit the Tower, separated from the image by the thickness of the walls against which I am leaning, that suddenly I see it after the fact and for the first time. Which means that perhaps up close, very close, without anything separating us, I would not have withstood receiving its truth without the mantle in which already I cloak it. I see myself leaning against the Tower as against the most maternal body in the world, gripped by this double revelation, that of the Image, in which I recognize the portrait of my destiny, and that of this long inert night that for forty years has kept me in its cave. I see that I have not yet described this image. For days I have been interrogating myself, not at all as to whether or not this image is true, for there is no doubt, but so as to know how, when, by what detours I will finally manage to tear it free from the tufts of resistance that hold me back by tangling around the feet, the legs of my thoughts right on the verge of the confession. I am not far from it I know, it seems to me I am held back a page away from it, all it would take I say to myself is one hour, but I'm forced to observe that my mind is as if incarcerated in a cell of incalculable obstinacy. I could sometimes almost weep from rage, from shame as well. It is true, probably, that this extreme difficulty in letting itself be described, simply named, can often be observed for scenes that or with persons who reappear after years of being forgotten or locked up. Everything then happens as if the one that appears or else the archeologist of vaults and crypts felt a vexing sadness, the fear of losing by manifesting the strange and pernicious pleasures that ooze in the crypt. It is so dark, one thinks one is going to give up the unplumbable darkness for a little limited light. We are not sure we want to share what is a true treasure even with ourselves. I digress

– Your brother is a hero! my brother flings at me while advancing between me and my tergiversation. He passes by barefoot, totally naked, wet, buoyed up by pride and while I am crouching beneath a burrow of paper, my heart stunted, I see him enlarged by his courage. – I took a swim, he tells me, and it was a noble and admirable swim that he alone had the honor of taking on this freezing day shunned by frightened would-be swimmers. How not to receive this letter from Destiny? The hero is the one who dives into his originary pool, be it sea, pond, lake, abyss of dreams, dungeon. The hero is the one who dives headfirst into heroism and gives himself the frigid baptism. The hero is the prisoner who frees himself from the prison of which he is the inventor by break-ing down his own walls. So, I say to myself, everything is in the secret of the crypt. One only gets out of it through the violence of some magic. Dive!

It is a window on sufferance. One can still see rather clearly the frame of the bars outlined above the fireplace on the right-hand side. One sees only those metal squares cut out against a grayish remainder of faraway light. It sums up the prison and every prison cell, and it is the whole universe. These iron bones that replace forests, streets, ports, churches, there it is: being; it is all that is left of the world for the pris-oner. Of the prisoner himself. The bones of the soul of the prisoner.

To the left against the chimney stands the tall naked stem of a bush that stretches its thin arms barely dressed in two leaves and two or three large pale roses uncertain as memo-ries. According to me, this is the Prisoner's Dream. The Dreamer is no more. What remains of the Prisoner turns empty sockets circled by the bars toward the slender and gracious body of the vegetal angel. I would imagine this behind the bars.

There reigns over the fireplace wall a grayish moldy silence, gnawed at by scars and the swear words of the generations that have trampled this tiny mausoleum century after century until its debris today.

Here where meditation lived is the office of Forgetting. The burial chamber of the brain. The site of the sacrifice. Of necessity, one has to do a little killing in the house, some evacuation. So, the drainpipe for the cruelties, the closet of relegations, was this small room, hidden away, contiguous with the library devoured by cannibalistic passions, I say to myself. From generation to generation visitors will come to satisfy their needs in what was perhaps a garden for the master a paradise to console hell, a rosebush to liberate a captive soul.

And for forty years I passed in front of the gallery of Montaigne's soul and I saw only the claw marks, the shreds of the wall's skin, the incurable lacerations of the body, the leprosies and not the fruits. But one day when I hastily leave the Tower alone in my solitude, and while I am leaning against its chest, a memory of an airshaft comes back to me, vague at first, then getting more precise little by little then a thunderbolt and with dizzying amazement I recognize the bars of my grate, the one on which the whole construction of my childhood stands and I remember that I was born from a prison and a freedom

– The one that had the frescos? Do you remember them? Several times I question my brother, in the kitchen while he is doing the dishes, in the doorway, if he doesn't remember in that room who knows if the image won't come back in the stairwell, or if it is not the heron who seems to await him in order to fly off as soon as he tries to approach it.

25

– Do you remember them?

– Hardly at all. Isn't it the first one? The one where Michael brings down the dragon?

– It's the last one, I say. And barely visible. It's all faded. The dragon brings me down. A few vague modifications of the colors in the background?

– Notice, notice, says my brother, this nothing is interesting. I remember nothing whatsoever.

Suddenly this window on sufferance now seems to me more powerful, more powerfully secret, more ineffaceable than all the rest of the Tower's heart of hearts. All I can see now is this screen. Remainder of remainder. Someone was tortured

The creator was assassinated, there was an ordinary murder, a little pillaging by vultures driven by natural law, man carcassing his own greatness. Here where flowed the spring for all the people's thirsts the usual poison has been spread around. The fireplace is dead. Spite and hatred make ashes of all the fire that flamed for him.

– Who?

Of a marvelous room, in Montaigne's psychical apartment where grow the eternally new and clear thoughts of the master who observes the goings-on of the world and gives them names that watch over the truth, which he had literally painted, illustrating his walls, I have no doubt, with the most significant scenes of the thinking passions, of his philosophical chapel, unique in the world, whose book I would have so wished to decipher, for it is here, here, the very heart of his library, they have left us but the ruined debris, of an orchard they have spared a branch to stoke our regret, of the history of humanity to whose secret I would so like him to lead us there remains the ghost of a jail, a grate that floats detached from the scene of which it used to be the gaze and the prophetic mask. Who? To whom alone did Montaigne speak alone, in his heart? Of freedom and death? Which words, which thoughts, miseries and commiserations, which struggles between lights and shadows? Near a garden or perhaps in its center, the visor of a vaulted cell. He lives with this scene carved in his chest, he bears a cruelty alongside the road scented with books and the sky plowed with sentences that teach him tirelessly to live tirelessly, it suffers side by side, what is freedom, the body in prison? If he or she, the prisoner, had known that of all his or her punishment the iron carcass would alone be the idiotic monument. They never left each other, nothing and no one were ever closer to the Spirit of the Tower and everything is erased except for the remainder. The Liberary and the Prison. The Jail and the Garden. Ruins and Life. The sublime excrements of an ancient mind. Hard sometimes, sometimes loose. Or else it is his self-portrait. Portrait of Montaigne in either bad condition or good condition: either wholly good or wholly bad. He always made one feel the whole of his inclinations and his affections. What he couldn't express by mouth he will have signaled to it pointed it out with his finger and to the eye leaving nothing to be surmised. I have lost my friend, I say to myself, he has been torn from me into a thousand contrary faces, after they had lacerated and tagged his true face, says Montaigne to himself, he alone enjoyed my true image and he takes it away. That is why I decipher myself so curiously. These brief signs here will suffice for those who are discerning, and will lead you to find the rest by yourself.

Verum animo satis haec vestigia parva sagaci
Sunt, per quae possis cognoscere cetera tute

Poor stolen vestiges. Poor vestiges of the poor vestiges of truth. A poverty that makes them more desirable to me like the reflection of the ungraspable, the sign that flees from the prisoner nothingness. And it is the very Vision of the secret. Look, he murmurs. I am the one who is not St

27

Michael bringing down the dragon. I am the one brought down, the one hanging from the threads where life crosses with death. And at the moment I turn to look it disappears. In vain I exert my discerning arts on the decomposing wall. I am ruined. The strange marriage arrested: which was perhaps the essence of the Essay.

Where? In the lowest reaches of Rome perhaps, the only universal city in common, he thinks, which possesses the power of evocation to an infinite degree since one cannot walk there without setting foot on the imprint of some history. He will have put Rome the Ruin par excellence in his boudoir. Having brought it back stuck to the leather of his shoes.

The powers of the ruin enchant me. I am in the state of passion of the Great Dreamers that my uncle Freud talks about, who having been nourished their whole lives at the breasts of Dream see themselves brutally weaned. One can find no greater cruelty than this surgery operated on the very lips that stretch out blindly toward the expected spurt of milk, as if some Evil wanted to withdraw Life at the living spring. It is an uprooting of light, the Dream is ripped from the brain with pincers. The tortured one is granted the bitter chance of powerlessness. He is left the ruins to chew over. For nothing in the world would the Weaned Dreamer give up this pale pain. You can believe me: *I know all about this*. There was a world in this tower, there was a Book in this head, of this immense Earth, I am left with two verses. I live on the milk of mourning. Eyes empty, vertebrae rusty, the bony sequestration of a humanity who was Montaigne's unknown lady friend, that is what serves me as the sun in the dungeon, the great open eye that I think I see contemplate the enchanted reader in his library, and scatter on the pages from which he makes his honey its inexhaustible golden beam.

Toward the end, the mystery of living is so strong that a timid little nothing keeps it flourishing.

So I go down to witness my mother's rising and on the waxed tablecloth there is the reflection of paradise, her psalm: "I slept until 8.00. I was nice and warm. I got up. I took away the papers from under my potty. I am having my coffee. Everything is fine. Happiness is assured by half a brioche. A flower has kindly come out on the left-hand branch of the magnolia. This little white pill is enemy #1. Cortisone it's called. Half-enemy half-friend. No one knows who is going to win. Everything is just fine."

My strength has gone but I am still there, says my mother the Tower. I contemplate, with the sad exultation of the visitor pierced through by the mad beauty of a painting that he was born to receive and that he will forever be unable to translate into any language, this immense pittance from which she makes all her days into events, this contentment that is her radiant art. This Tower that is my mother, eroded where she stands, furrowed, perpetual, is one of those monuments of an unreal reality, at the feet of which my sentences come crashing down. It is in a sort of dream that I see her shining before me. I touch her. She is altogether real to the touch but indescribable, calm and straight like the little blue Virgin, but warm, knotted, white and flushed with the Cortisone color that delicately poisons her cheeks. I feel her marbled left arm, gloved in a skin so excessively thin that one is amazed at finding it still standing after so much inclemency.

Our strength is gone. Remains Strength. It passes through the navel of the Dream. One doesn't enter, one is born dreamed, one is navigated, one is beached.

Mama has never seen the Tower.

My mother has never come to Montaigne.

29

I have never offered to take my mother to see the Tower of Montaigne

My mother has never expressed the desire to see the Tower of Montaigne.

When I am at Montaigne I think ardently of my mother who is awaiting my return while thinking of me. That is to say of her daughter. That is to say of her mother.

This is my ideal of ideals I say to myself.

It is a mixture of haste and eternity

Death smiles at me from both sides –

I think only of it, of her

I think I remember that one summer, a very long time ago, I asked my mother if she would like to come with me to the Tower of Montaigne, it may take two hours on the highway, the path leading to the extraordinary look-out is narrow and bumpy, but at the end one is saved, I said, it would be tiring, but in my opinion she could withstand the ordeal, despite her very advanced age that already was more than ninety years. Naturally if she came on this expedition I would be occupied with her alone.

In writing this I am trying to get close to some charm that escapes me.

A mist covers my memory as soon as I want to know what it is that acts on me coming from the Tower

It seems to me that I have never really confided my most secret heart of hearts. I have perhaps already said all this in another scene. Never has my mother seemed to me as flamboyant and adorable as at this Distance where from the Tower I see her in me living twice: by being and by being-still –

I hear my mother's voice call me from the depths of the world. The thread of thin breaking dry voice rises trembling beneath the sands: "Where are you?" moans the thread of sounds. I hear the distress, and the distress does not hear me. I cry into the microphone: "I'm coming!" Oh, vain speech, deceptive present, this Imcoming is swallowed by the tongues of nothingness. "Wherareyou" flutters the whimper, meager cry of the blind curlew. This is the picture of our new age: I hear her not hear me. In vain she cries, in vain I cry and although she does not hear me I cry anyway because perhaps she'll hear me otherwise.

– Whereryou! Whereryou!

– She's lost something again and she is still losing being, I say to my brother. It is perhaps the last time, crawls an aborted and livid thought, but I give it no respect.

In every book there is a chapter where I force myself to go to court. It would be a confessional if I were kneeling. I submit to the interrogation. Are you sure that you are not in sin? To prefer writing over your mother? No I say to myself. The more I write the more I love to love Mama I love to sin by this love. Are you sure you are not lying? No, I say. But how will I be. Wherever I turn I kill myself and I adore

In every book there is in a chapter a letter that I think I am addressing to my mother, in which I would announce to her that after this book I will no longer go to Montaigne instead of staying with her, of taking a walk in the supermarket, I will no longer get lost the whole day chasing after things that take me down paths that do not recognize death's approach, and that in the end I do not write.

This letter sings to me, then disappoints me. I want to write it: it will say: I do not write.

My mother weeps: she has lost *Schirm*, the umbrella. She weeps for her umbrella. She confides her misery to the telephone. To lose *Schirm* the umbrella is serious, no one can deny it. It is a non-possibility. Short of losing one's head,

31

nothing worse can happen. Her umbrella is her. Where? I say. She had it and she had it no longer. My mother weeps for herself. I am going to put a notice in the elevator! she says. – Why not? I say. I feel ready for every sort of exorcism. I have trouble seeing how my mother was able to get along without her umbrella without which she can't take a step. We have thus arrived in the region of the Improbable.

– It's a touch of Old Age, a blow from Old Man time! says my mother. Sore at heart we wonder who this Old Man is. According to my mother it's cousin Albert. She had gone to Albert's. – I was very surprised to see him so bent over. He can't see anything. He can't hear anything. I didn't under-stand a word he said. So it's the end. – So it's finished – Does my mother suspect Albert is behind the blow? It can only be something totally impossible, aberrant, unbelievable, because she herself cannot lose or forget or do without Schirm the Umbrella. – I have never lost anything, says my mother. It's my fault. I had it in the street. All at once, it's no longer there. *Selbst ist der Mann.* I should be autonomous. It is thus my fault. – I'm coming, I cried. She is at the door with *Schirm.* – Here it is! says the little voice. It wasn't there anymore. It is there. It is a blow from Hiatus, my mother's Satan.

That is how one dies.

I am dying. It is a natural misfortune. One says dying, not really knowing how. In this very moment I am dying a little, which doesn't prevent me from living. One says: I am dying. Then, one gets delayed. The way in which my mother gets more and more delayed fills me with a respectful astonish-ment. It's because my mother's story is taking place at present in a country where the hours are much slower than ours. The bedroom might well be a garden: it's because my mother cultivates the closet, the dresser, the little table with medita-tion. Everything is thought through, worked out, the delicate and laborious gestures are reflected, sometimes corrected. A true country of luxury. Beings and things endowed with an unprecedented and considerable importance attract a mysterious light, which may be nothing other than the gleam of visibility. You should see Going-to-Bed. Every piece of clothing is the object of religious care. Blouse, pants, underclothes receive equal and singular treatment. The individual, in all its guises, is honored. Thus these objects which for me would be a common outfit are filled by a sort of soul, the pajamas are recognized as The Pajamas. The idea occurs to me that perhaps my mother sees in these idols of wood and cloth the faces of ancient beings with whom her old age sympathizes

Dying? A way of living.

I am dying of your old age. What your old age gives me: a terrible Youth. The New Life. She barely sleeps. She is acute, radiant, heart-rending, passionate about the successive blooming of flowers. I am living on your old age. I follow it. I walk at dawn. On the path everything is being born. Invitation to being. Meanwhile I walk with your death at my heels. It escorts me on the days I will be cut in half. The Follower looks like you in advance, it is your blurry, pale image, or not an image at all, your squeaking presence as hatchling fallen from the nest

The Satans are everywhere. They bear their names on their insidious faces. Actually I see their bare feet wiped in dirt more often than their faces, which are always indecisive but often pensive and cold. But Cybele, the mother crowned in towers, accompanies me.

I am living on you, I say. What we cook up! They are the basins of dreams. Up to thirteen.

One morning, soul-bankrupt, I empty out, what left me was a well-made dream, long and complicated like a world from which I drew a feeling of satisfaction, I had done my work, I had overcome the obstacles it gave me a restful sensation, duty accomplished, and at that very moment the dream was taken away from me like this: like a rug one pulls from beneath the head's feet, bam, bam! like a tapestry of life folded up in a flash it was a head theft like the ground of the world taken from me under the brain, quickly *extracted*, at the very moment I was at peace in my dream, it was the evening, I was going to savor a nap, unsuspecting, bang, nothing left, my head had been cut off and thrown like a headless fish into the dreamless day, pardon me for writing this to you, wrote Freud to Antigone, I had a shock of despair. Someone kidnapped the analysis from me, the faceless demonic. In the thick darkness I tried to retrieve the traces, but after the first brutal subtraction, the last operation, I thought, the Erasure of the Dream was doing its work. The demons are so frightening because they are Night Forces, Wills bent on Harm that cannot be localized. They have the *atrocious* ability to destroy us so precisely that one feels pierced through by the very blackness that has entered into us. All that I had left was the *certainty of the loss*, a certificate of loss of Dream, that is all I could put down. Instead of the narrative of a dream, a death certificate. So that is what you make me feel, I say to Analysis, at least according to my interpretation, for I was addressing my mother standing behind me, – how did I manage to see her, the way one "sees" in a dream, she was not saying a word, she was at the age when I had adored her, I mean my age, around fifty. I had sworn to myself that I wouldn't complain, what else is new, evil is weary, and I literally broke into internal sobs. Notice it was also a tribute, a posthumous declaration of love to what or who is more myself than I, which had just *jilted* me

Oh, you who are the Dream to me, you who are so natural to me that I was able to feel myself the author of my mother – notice that I have nevertheless always been conscious of having as Psyche a soul that I owed to maternal love, I have always felt added on to myself by the admirably devoted Power that kept me above the abyss, that saved me from the River every day, I said, addressing with infinite nostalgia the one for whom and by whom I have lived and whose "death" has been, for the last few weeks, inflicted on me in full daylight, as if the time had come for reimbursing the debt. You've enjoyed yourself enough, go to the check-out counter. The counter is in very simple white wood. Its rough, natural, empty interior awaits me. I have arrived at the terminal of Analysis. Everyone must get off. I cannot with decency claim to help when my head is uninhabited ruins. Dreams flee my skull as if they already smelled the pestilential odor. Jofi also keeps away from my person. This withdrawal into a beyond, this ablation, this silence, and to top things off this disappearance the trace, the trace, the presence, in the air, beneath the earth, in the stairwells, everywhere I cannot go, of an ancient breath. She was the life of my life, I would say "my life" and it was she, you, I would say at dawn, like the primitives, who we are in secret, you who said to me Go, Dream, I who was your Dream and you the crowned Queen of towers who waited for me every night and came to open the ivory doors for me, it is thus This There that is happening to me, a There of exile, without return and without arrival, not only do you pull away the nights' great sheet as you depart, you leave me naked like a bone in the wind, and after that you are no longer in my days, my analytic clientele is vanishing, it is understandable and just that patients do not rush to see an analyst who receives no more letters from the Night, if I have only nights left, I am going to die of the desert.

Such a violent solitude opens its jaws of silence around me, to end this way, before the end, I have pity for myself: I have begun to write down my complaint. It is to you my daughter that I will leave this document; the word immortality is drained of life like me, but I cannot renounce what is left of this limited superstition. I "console" myself at this moment by foreseeing that you will read this narrative with the sadness of love. Here is the last secret (I have just discovered it): "This is how one dies." *I have experienced it. The apocalypse that has befallen me, I am sure of it, is the exact prefiguration of what is in principle absolutely hidden from us. Well, I, my darling daughter, I am dead. One dreams, one is very much alive. One "lives" in the heart of a great dream with its continents, empires, charming domestic scenes, powerfully naïve years with their seasons that make us believe in the miracle of continuity how beautiful is that existence in which one believes with an unambivalent belief, I have been as happy as a dog, in a life freed from conflict with myself, from conflict with civilization, I knew an existence perfect in itself, I had some years, I was lodged in a humid and cool husk, I watched the human antlions bark nearby around an image for which they were prepared to shed every kind of blood, I went to the cinema and I saw all the myths, I saw the hidden plots themselves that drive kings to the summits and then into the abysses, all those dreamers who don't know they are dreaming, all those living ones who think they are stronger than the dead. And suddenly, there occurred an ex*traction, *a traction that had a mad strength, thought, the world, are quickly folded up from under the living, the reel of the scene starts over, rolls up with the tautness of a spring beneath the brain of the living one whose self is quite simply wiped out from one moment to the next. The tyrant remains as obscure as his name, the most obscure of all etymology. It cannot be studied. In a great Mourning that lasts a fraction of a second, an immense white heartbroken mourning, in a sad sigh cut off from the sadness that has no more subject, no more master, one has lost, I have lost, I no longer lose, there is nothing more I have been eclipsed. If you want to know how when I am dead as you look at my disaffected body stretched out like a meager coffin on the couch, I will have left you in the desk drawer the story of my martyrdom. This time I will not wake up complaining bitterly of* *having been robbed during the night. Also consult what the etymological dictionaries report about the word* tirer, *as in* soutirer, *as in* to extract. *You will see them bear witness to their impotence and their ignorance. – What are you waiting for? Jofi thinks – "Why live if you can be buried for 10 dollars?" I found this "advertisement" in the* New York Times. *It's exactly what the dog who lives in me thinks. I confess that I would pay dearly to have the vision of the last dream. Unless it has already passed in front of me?*

– Do you still have a lot of ink in your head? My mother sticks her head into the doorway of the study. She wants to tell me a story. She has the face she puts on when she has a story. – I'm writing, I say. There is still some ink. – So here is the story. – No, I say, no story. – And you? You have some ink? In my head, there is no ink. In my head I have: lead.

She looks at me. Her nose is running.

– Later, I say.

It seems to me that this is how I shift the limits of life and death.

She has never been so beautiful, I say to myself. It's not an illusion I am making up. My mother crowned with towers accompanies me. And in the next room, the Satans are cooking something up.

While I am at Montaigne, my mother is in *The Plague*.

Everything is in the End. The End is always in Books. What we don't see, Books know. They keep the secret. Everything is written. We read them, they tell us everything and we understand nothing. All the same, they give us the Signal. Books read us and understand everything that we think behind thought. When we think we are choosing books, we are under the Illusions they have prepared for us: they were waiting, sitting on their tripod in their oracular silence, for us to obey the fate they have in store for us. These beings whom we acquire so we think for next to nothing are our dry nurses and our friends before any friendship. With these dead who don't forget us we enter into conversations that take place only in vast chambers of silence. It is thus as alerted living beings, having duly received the ticket for death, already somewhat specters but very intimidated that we ask them for their opinion, these dead ones who graze in the fields of paper. How is it, there, how do things work, a thousand eager and naïve questions crowd against the electric fence, and a little ashamed of this impatience, fearing we will be surprised and reprimanded for curiosities deemed premature, illegitimate, immodest, we act as if we were interested only as scientific researchers in the bizarre charms of dying.

The Book that chose Freud to finish the year 1939 is *La Peau de chagrin* (*The Wild Ass's Skin*). This is the Book by which Freud chose to let himself be chosen so as to have done with summer. It is the first tome that comes effortlessly into the hand he stretches toward the bookshelf in the sitting room to the right upon entering. It so happens it is precisely *La Peau de chagrin*, a book that has the faculty of causing one to forget it no sooner has it been read, a little like a Dream: as long as one is living there, as long as one is staying in a lovely hotel, one cannot dream of a more brilliant, obsessive and indisputable reality. One is captivated. As soon as the End arrives, everything vanishes, there is barely enough time to read the conclusion because time melts in front of one's eyes, it no sooner presents itself than the last page turns pale, lets out a cry and disappears. One wakes up completely stripped, empty, emptied, without end. Freud has a hole. He no longer remembers the name of the patient of the *Peau de chagrin* who had nevertheless consulted him during a first visit to Vienna. In order to camouflage this hole, which embarrasses him, he calls him "our hero." If one had asked him which book he desired to read recently, he would have wanted to say *La Peau de chagrin*, but it's possible this book's title escaped him. He is struck by the Coincidence: *La Peau de chagrin* is exactly the book he needs. According to him it is the book of shrinking. The patient flees life for fear of dying. On the other hand *La Peau de chagrin* seems to him exactly the book it would be better not to read. So if he had not found it while groping and totally by chance, it's possible that the Forgetting of the name would have deterred him from asking for it. There is some Demon in this story. What he would have fled surrenders to him. It looks like a Temptation. Having never been superstitious, it's with humility and precision that he notes the several cases in which he might acknowledge his Temptations and Superstitions. Is he not now being dragged into those strange regions of which there are no reports because once the travelers go behind the curtain of gray or maybe black vapors, but which all seem equally white, they forget to take notes, are stricken with indolence and seem no longer to care about leaving accounts that might have enlightened posterity? In his log book he wondered if it is the last book that he would have read. So it would be the Book that awaited him? He could make it wait. Drag out the reading? There are dozens of ways to do that. This book resists every effort of diversion. There is something that prevents you from getting rid of it. Moreover, was it a real Book? Or rather the Book of Destiny? When one would begin to read a certain Book one would know that it's the End. What bothers him is the Dream that astounded him that night. He wonders if it is the last of the Dreams. It was about a visitation that he did not expect and to which he cannot pose the least shred of resistance: it will have entered by the staircase that leads from the infernal world up to the man weakened by age or illness.

A True Novel, that is the title of this dream. It would thus have presented itself in the guise of a novel truer than nature.

39

In this dream he goes to the *notary*. The notary comes from: on the one hand the philosophical novels of Balzac, in which these characters provide the link with real Society; on the other hand a testamentary impulse whose recurrence in his head Freud has vaguely remarked so as to push it back behind the door. He forgets the word notary. He asks the character in question to find him a new comfortable little house. To pay he will sell the old one. It's there at the "notary's" that he meets the Saint in the dress of Vapors. Things go very quickly. In a second, he recognizes her beneath her veils: it is a Death which has some charm. A Viennese woman. He should have guessed. She makes him an amorous proposition. Naturally, it will be a dance and it's been a long time since he waltzed. He wonders who leads. She is upon him. But he's the one who undoes his clothes. Everything seems real. The Saint has breasts like toys. She caresses him. He is astonished. He thinks underneath her, as is his habit: what would upset him would be to give up mastery. It would really beat all to start loving death or to find himself feeling no hostility, no mistrust and even surreptitiously in complicity with its audacity, her audacity. This would be the first time that his eternal dream of sovereignty met a more sovereign sovereignty than his. He realizes that he is mentally pronouncing Louvereign. So here I am in Rome and once again I'm suckling the She-Wolf, the "Louve," who makes me king. That's why the little pointed udders. It's my turn to nurse, he exclaims, still in thought. No one will say that the great Freud did not know how to pleasure the Wolf Queen. He notes with a certain satisfaction the incestuous dimension that enhances the excitement of this scene: the Queen and the She-Wolf who is also the Virgin or Minerva if she has the air of Authority is of an age to be his daughter. He is himself proof that ego is ageless and without obstacle. That's not bad, he says to himself, for my age. The unconscious is still young. If only the world knew. To begin with it reverses the roles into the opposite. Here he is now stretched out on top of her. He wants to want the inevitable, no one will say that she made of him her conquest. He will thus feel a certain pleasure in embracing her. The essential thing is to be able to want one's own defeat, he calculates, if he must renounce conquering her he wants at least to desire an exaltation in renouncing, he will be the inventor and poet of the triumph of powerlessness. Is it a passing fancy? he wonders. An adventure with no tomorrow? They get up. She is indecipherable. He acts detached: it's late, he says, I have to go home. She doesn't seem eager to restrain him. He remains on his guard: either the Saint is a Circe, or else she's a mystical functionary, she carries out her duties with neutrality, according to a scenario she respects and that is not shared with the dancer. He had always imagined a final encrypted, fabulous scene, with spectacular apparitions either sylphs or nixies. Or else gnomes like the ones that come out of the body of the Prisoner who sleeps his Prison in a dream of escape.

Schwind's painting comes up apropos to form a diptych with what he is just then living through. As an artist of dream Freud congratulates himself on this marvelous find. This dream definitely promises to be a masterpiece. It is indeed endlessly augmented on all sides by magnificent doubles, with illustrations from Freud's collection, which is itself also double: there is the collection in the proper sense which is at home (the one he was getting ready to sell so as to buy a virgin home) and the virtual collection in which abound the memorable holdings of many galleries and civilizations. The library of the unconscious beats the British Museum, he says to himself. Well, this *Schwindchen Bild* – as he calls it in his notebooks, which is a manner of surreptitiously appropriating the object that he cannot consciously make his own – is the very image, something like the anticipatory model, the

41

prophecy already realized in the smallest details, of what is happening to him at this very moment, that is, seventy-five years after the premiere of his own final scene represented by this Moritz von Schwind, a predecessor who will thus have been inspired by the spirit of predestination. One needn't look elsewhere for the explanation. The painting is now placed to the right of the dream, in a frame separated by a ribbon of gold, but it is bathed by the same light, a painted band of an almost supernatural radiance, whose source seems to be the starry heart from which desires are launched. The Dreamer is awake. He is the Prisoner. The Prison does not prevent the visit from a beautiful woman, still young, serious, maternal, who floats above him. Let us return to the main action: "It is late," he says, "I must leave." He is in shirt-sleeves. "My drawers are in the next room," he says. That's what holds him back. He prefers not to go out half-naked. Something knows that, once through the door, reality and its conventions are once again in force. The neutral Queen tells him that she is going to look for this piece of clothing. Left alone, he analyzes: this situation causes him neither joy nor anxiety. A surprise merely, and what surprises him is the erotic but warrior dimension revealed in this liaison with the She-Wolf. He is not in love with her, he doesn't feel moved. Nor is he taken over, obsessed as he would be by a mistress who belonged to him. No quivering of transference. He does not wish to possess her as he would wish to possess a painting. Finally it is indeed the very *painting* of destiny that he desires. He quite recognizes himself in this. He is delighted to have seen Death, it rather pleases him that she is a Queen, thereby gratifying his inclinations, which were always aristocratic. But the woman, no, he doesn't feel himself coming to life again in her. She is taking a long time. Finally he gets impatient. Has she forgotten him? Is he going to be a prisoner of appearances? No. Go out half-naked, if he is seen, he's awake. He

42

slips on a long robe, beautiful as a stretch of river, goes out quickly, enters into the next room. There he finds the Queen grappling with one of his old dead, a young man, whose face reminds him of a friend whom he stopped loving in the past and whose jealousy was never extinguished. She snubs him sharply and strongly. The other clearly sees thereby that mistrust of what she has in store for him in the future is not justified. She is on his side. Woman-mistress, he says to himself. Naturally at no point did he envision that his death could be a man, despite the noun's gender in his language, but that she might have a streak of virile strength is a fact he does not dispute. She joins him, gives him his jerkin, neither pressures nor pleads with him to stay. For her he is hers. He however is worried. "I want secrecy," he says. What would Mary or Martha say? All the women whose names begin with M? "Above all," he says, "I fear that the little one will worry. He looks like he understands. I don't want him to know," he says. "Even if now I think he doesn't give a damn. I'm afraid of hurting him." The little one is the one he loves, it's he, it's the child in him who is playing in the ruins, it's his genius, the ego he secretly admires, the same as Shakespeare, the same enfant terrible as the Wolfgang who throws his whole family out the window, while laughing aloud, the sublime scamp to whom he vows an unavowable worship, the same whom his mother has always adored in all his forms, the one of whom he is jealous since he would so like to be sure he himself is the one chosen by the divinities who are guardians of the seeds of humanity. He has worked so hard for this: the irrational hope more powerful than his reason that the little one will be immortal. It is for the child in him that he regrets being the old man whose mistress is Death. She is with him in crowds, she talks in his ear. For her it's just a matter of days. She doesn't hurry him because it's already done.

43

Moritz von Schwind, *The Prisoner's Dream*

FREUD DREAMS NO MORE

These last weeks, he notes, I have been as stripped of dreams as my face is now stripped of beard. It no longer grows, it falls off in patches like shreds of moss toasted by radium. A life without dreams is not a life, I say to myself. For someone whose whole life has been nourished by the material and machines of the world to-be-read it is to be condemned to die of starvation. But one never knows with dreams. Certain dreams kill us. The dreamer might be stopped before a white Curtain stretched the whole height of a wall. A livid white like a petrified veil has replaced the marvelous screen on which the film of Life was playing. It's a breakdown. One waits for the projection to continue. Tension mounts in the crowd that pushes against the base of the wall. Later people lose faith. They no longer believe that the flow of images will start running again. They leave one after the other. A terrible, dark feeling of abandonment rises in the veins of the Dreamer. He begins to guess that he is now nothing more than this immense silent shroud. And no one for the anxiety?

We are always thinking elsewhere, I was thinking a year ago, but that's provided there is an elsewhere, I thought. In our powerlessness, we are forced to accept everything destiny has in store for us, I had written to Ernest, on March 7, but that's provided destiny has something in store. Without an elsewhere I am in a state of ouster. The Giant anxiety of the Worst encircles me. I wrote that on October 23, 1938. I am threatened with death. Naturally it's not about the inevitable end. It's about the end before the end. There is no other death than the death that knocks at the door before death. And the hell of hell, who knows that?

E quindi uscimo per riveder le stelle.

I was singing that thirty years ago in Rome in the Roman columbarium of the catacombs where I spent the night all alone with the dead. I was alive then, although enclosed underground. In vain I repeat the last verse to myself in order to get out of Hell: this verse is dead. It is but a worm of dead words without stars. I have often spent the night with my dead and the bones of the dead, I slept in Rome's columbarium, it is cold and dark there, you might think you were dead if Dreams were not watching over you. Lately, when at the end of the book I exit Hell: no stars. Am I outside? Am I still there? I see nothing anymore. No one sees me. I don't dream any more than a bone does. Dreams are letting go of me. It is the Great Fear. Thus both worlds are leaving me. Were the nightworld in which I have always found refuge to be withdrawn from me would I have nowhere to live? Thus I am dying. The way one dies: alive. I die myself. Tomb tumbling – into ruins. I am ruined. I said to Anna: now not only am I good for nothing during the day, but this means that I am no longer there *to myself*. I am reduced to Zero. I don't even remember "myself." I know, from knowledge and not from "feeling," that under the same name as me there used to live someone strong, who gave up on nothing and found replacements, who took the brunt of storms on his chest but knew how to grab hold of their manes with the right hand. He has been. He was brilliant. And very resourceful: he played the event under many signatures: Papa, Moses of Ithaca, Ulysses the Egyptian, Your Sigm., Dr Sigm. Freud, Dr Freud, Your Sigmund, Your old new father-in-law, your tender and hostile transference, Your faithful Singe Traum and so on.

It was said of him that he was tireless and that was true. I am the void, the nullity, the flat, the extinguished being, bald Samson, someone else. The only thing still alive in me is the sting of terrible, desperate jealousy regarding the one I will never be again. Farewell! It is awful to be the dead one of the living one. A terrible fear instead of assurance, poise, repose, he steadfastly consoled his friends, finally he used to say I would have shown you that everything is foreseeable, no death resists the attentions of interpretation, I used to say, I was ready when I was thirty years old, when evening came I was saved. A riverbank, a cigar, a little Lethe, in a flash Faust is on the other side. An emperor. The boat in which I used to take my seat to cross the night while breathing a sigh of relief is now nothing but a bed, a piece of narrow wood, on which the empty sack is laid, me. Now nothing disturbs the shadows. Not one traveler. No visits. The prodigious peoples who made up my kingdoms have disappeared like an unknown race. After all I am not going to beg my way into the nights inhabited by my friends. My night is now nothing but a heavy and moldy wall next to my old stiff side. If I can no longer suckle I will not be able to survive crossing the day of this year from which I have nothing more to expect except the doctor and illness. To be sure, I say to Anna, I still happen upon a charming sentence from time to time. I can still feel joy ignite upon contact with a sublime line of Shakespeare, which was

47

still simmering beneath the forgetfulness where I had kept it. I can thus still feel. But in me nothing moves. Everything is Job, it is as if my flocks had never existed. There's an old man who chews on cinders in the sleep box without dreams. Alone three very small worms come and go frenetically in the shoe box. My paralysis abhors them. The furious urge comes upon me to crush them. An urge without body without muscles. I take them for what they are: the derision of dreams, the conquerors of Yorick. Last evening October 29 I asked Anna to stay. I was afraid of the bed. Of this fraud, this enmity, this trap. To be betrayed every night why? by whom? God has stopped keeping me company, I said to Anna. I cannot feed myself. I have fallen into dust. It's not that there are no dreams. It's that they are torn from me the instant I go to touch them. I reach out my hand, lips, and: dust. One wants me to die of my hunger. One wants to wean the old Dreamer. One wants to break him on the wheel, torture him where he has conquered, they want to gouge out the eyes of the mole. And naturally memory says to me: you used to know who *one* was. But it is dust that answers from now on in the debris of me. I used to make it a point never to complain, that was when I was doctor master of my house, today the man is nothing except horror, people lament, it's better than nothing, Job does not surrender without pitying himself.

I have decided to pitch camp in the state I am in. Anna as army, asleep on the sofa. I have beside my good cheek the green notebook, pens. All night dreams paraded by. Mockeries of nothingness. I might have been a mummy but still I disengaged my fingers from my bandages, to pinch a paw, a hair. I noted down accidents. Some glimmers. I wanted to call the one who is in the forbidden house and whose name I don't know. I thought he could, if he heard me, come to me, before me. I was walking in the dark, that's saying a lot, I was pushing my body beneath a vault along the miles that were two yards long, immovable crawling on my back or stomach, for hours I had as horizon and goal the titanic crossing over this tiny parade, I saw myself, I was the petrified one, the carcass stuck in the gums of the pavement, a worm as big as an ant wriggled on my forehead causing me a cruel pang of humiliation. I came into the sunlight completely naked – I must have jettisoned my overcoat, my shoes, my hat, my briefcase containing the book that is going to appear this week and whose title I have totally forgotten, I know it is "difficult," that's the word our enemies use, but I am the last one able to defend it at the moment – at the price of the most costly effort that I have ever made as far as I remember, the thrust of a shark's tail, what is called the energy of despair, one is no longer a man but one wants to continue the race, whereupon I let the telephone fall on a pile of garbage and shards. I picked it up, it was all dusty. I blew on the dusty grains, a breath so weak one could cry, even the grains of dust withstand me. In such conditions, impossible to call the dream.

All night I struggled, noted down everything that was happening, the complete history of my defeats, had there been even a worm to keep me company I would have greeted it, cherished it. But the worms persecuted me.

Anna thinks that perhaps it is Pity who keeps dreams away from me. Who knows, she thinks, if this Angel who sees everything may not be trying to spare me the pain of seeing myself in the last throes and perhaps even the last one. But I am still the remains of a man, that is, a dreadful pain that demands to know its causes.

Nur wenn wir im Kot uns fanden,

So verstanden wir uns gleich, I say to Anna

As Heine said, we understand ourselves better when we're in the shit.

This here shit, I say, is a bottomless pain, and that is all I have left to explore.

On October 30, the struggle continues, everything continues, the shit continues the pain continues, the neuralgia continues, the bone of will is the only element of my being that emerges from the shit. Armed guard this night. I visited my camp. Placed the green notebook as sentinel. A little less afraid than yesterday all the same. The reason: it's the action. If it is written that I must sink into the fathomless lead, I will go down standing, holding the pain in my hand. Tensed. Lookout. Towards midnight, I captured a first little dream. At least there are dreams. My avidness. I am salivating abundantly. I note down the least curtain. Curtain. Color: none. Pillowcase. My feeling of infinite poverty poor poor feeling. My poor one. I munch on the poor word "pauvre." My German complained in French. I couldn't say the word poor in German. I understood that I managed to take pity only when in foreign shit. Noted *poor* in English I can feel sorry for my skull. Continued the night path. Dagger blow: a great dream has escaped. Perfect homicide. Nothingness sticks out its tongue. Hamlet has a hole. What was it called this skull? One will never know. I was pleased at the first dream, however small. The one in the middle I lost. I see myself still standing before the mirror dressed in a lined white shirt that hid my defects. In profile I was still handsome. The rest of the dream – withdrawn. A fear gripped me. I took up watching again. I had the green night notebook in my hand. I was on the lookout for the next one. I didn't hear it coming. Already it was there immense immensely sad, all of a sudden while I was wandering sadly between the sad curtains of mourning, I noticed that I was wandering in a dream. The dream depicted: the way I forget myself. I even forget the memory of my dog, poor memory of the dog that I am. Quick to arms! I know, the ghost comes back more than once in Act I

I am back on the rampart, *in the void*. Waiting for the revered ghost whoever it is. Let them come! Cramps, fatigue beyond fatigue, headache, discouragement, pains ear, nose, deceptive half-sleep, I struggle, I splash about like someone damned in the soup of nothingness, sad circus, I hear a thought down below that is trying to raise a filthy reply up to the rampart: "I surrender." That is not what I think. "Serpent!" I say. And at that moment, without my being aware of it, I was in a dream, in a manner quite as uncontrollable as when I am confined outside. And right away after that, I tear myself away from Acheron with the dream, I come safe out of the sea of *Kot* screaming with my mouth full of milk teeth, conqueror brought down at five o'clock avidly I noted noted noted (documents all in notebook S) I captured it whole, with its melancholy and its long message of distress. Advice: do not go back to sleep on these meager laurels.

November 1,1938. How I struggled this night. I almost failed. Exhausted, tense. Invisible, viscous spirits arose in me they said: let's drop it. And it's I nonetheless Sigmund who forced them to let go, they had planted their hysterical claws in my right arm, the little vampires, I unfastened them at one stroke like a bandage. Then at 4.30 came the long dream called: *let's not drop it.* A long day of ordeals in the form of a mountain gullied with holes, beginning with a struggle lasting several hours, an immense incessant effort to come back to dress myself correctly after having run out in a nightshirt just like that idiot Hanold, whom I've always been afraid of resembling in secret. It reminds me of the straitjackets at the Salpêtrière. The worst pain for a soul that has suffered from a body thrown in a dungeon: the feeling of being in the belly of a jacket. It's in this state that I set off on escape accompanied by an English gnome and a German gnome. We go for a long time, on a road that is more and more foreign and more and more white (see green notebook). I summarize. Descending undescendable mountainous dunes. Then exhausting climbs back up that lead to the stockade wall. There I have to get over the wall with a metallic ladder every step of which kills me. The dream declared then that it was called: Here is my Life. At the top one can't get through the slit. We call for help. I recognize the help who is distinguished, honorable, decorated: it's the grand pontiff of the School of Paris, the famous professor B., the Cuvier of skin diseases, a Pyrrhonian mind, specialist in desperate measures, poetic defender of Van Helmont's thesis according to which, since he claims there are secondary souls, called *archaea*, a man can still live after his death. The specialist recommends that I shrink as much as possible. Only way to get through the slit, which is as big as the jaws of a letterbox. That's medicine for you. That's when I notice to the right of the dream the end of the wall. All these unnecessary efforts taken to their extreme, I come back to earth. What a state I am in, my god. I was dust: I am earth. Still living after my death. Dream dictated to Anna. Each dream torn through great struggle from the jaws of hell. This will demand *all* my forces up to *the last* of them.

The Prisoner's Dream is hung in the gallery of "Children's Dreams."

I show my mother here a reproduction of Moritz von Schwind's painting, a reproduction of which Freud showed his audience in 1916 in order to illustrate his lecture on *Kinderträume*.

There is no other image in the book of "Children's Dreams." According to Freud, *The Prisoner's Dream* can have no other content except escape. That day Freud doesn't tell his audience a tenth of what he thinks: "every Dreamer is a prisoner who escapes."

– This Schwindian imagination, says Freud, is kept in the Schack Gallery in Munich, it thus exists in reality, under lock and key.

– As for me, I see someone who is going *up there* with a baby. What is hanging there? says my mother. In front of the wall, beneath the bars? It looks like a woman; unless it's a dog; who is a woman. And the one who is below, he is dreaming this perhaps?

– What is lovely, says Freud, is that the dream of a prisoner can have nothing other than *escape as content*

– And what is in the background? says my mother. You can't see it very well. She closes her right eye. Scrutinizes. His wife perhaps?

– It is a very neat stroke, says Freud, that the escape should be effected through the window and not through the door, for the ray of light that awakens the prisoner comes through the same window.

– I don't understand that, says my mother. There is a baby who is climbing here, to the bars in the background, you see? says my mother. Below it looks like an animal unless it's a woman. It's his dream probably. Full of children. All these dreams. They are his children

– The gnomes, says Freud, standing one above the other, represent the successive positions that he himself would have to assume

– Babies, says my mother, to pull himself up to the height of the window.

But yes, continues my mother, her right eye closed, it must be a woman down below. It's too religious for me, since they're floating in the air. It looks like a Mary.

I see that they are all enclosed because there are bars. He must be in prison there? Where are my glasses? It makes no difference with glasses. In the background, what is it? Another baby?

– If I am not mistaken, says Freud, if I am not attributing too much preconcerted design to the artist, if I am not mistaken – with or without my glasses, then, the uppermost of the gnomes, who is filing the bars, you see, which is what the prisoner would like to do. If I am not mistaken the uppermost of the gnomes is

– Another baby, says my mother.

– He has the features of the prisoner.

– The one who climbs all alone relying only on himself?

– The other one. The one who has pulled himself onto the others

– It makes no difference at all, says my mother.

And the woman who is floating. They are all locked up. So the children are climbing on this person who floats.

– Now, says my mother, I don't know if he is in prison or if he is dreaming all this. When you dream you don't know you're dreaming, so you're not dreaming. I notice he has a nice shirt with white sleeves. He must be in prison with all those bars. But he has a sofa. He's lying down on what? On a red coat? He sees all those children who are climbing one on top of the other. What should I say? He's locked up. Either he's in prison, or he's dreaming, so that he's in prison and he dreams he's in prison or else he imprisons himself while dressed, so that he must be in prison that's all, and he's dreaming. Or else it's the prison that's in his dream. – How do you know? I say. – Because it's not true: it's obvious says my mother that there are not a lot a children who are climbing over each other when you are in prison in reality. Although that may happen. Even though he has a fine white shirt. He must be in prison, that's all.

It's a man who is dreaming. Here is his dream: there is the sun that enters, and the children. He must really be locked up, the poor man.

This Moritz von Schwind, if he painted this, it's because he himself was in prison. He must have grandchildren at home. Perhaps everyone was in prison. The whole family. A real nightmare.

When I was in prison, it was a very amusing time, the company was good, we were well fed thanks to the madam of the brothel. One woman had a baby at her breast. Another had a miscarriage but I didn't get involved.

– It's like for Aeneas, says Freud. During his katabasis, there were moments when one could wonder if this whole story wasn't a dream? A dream of truth. That would mean that Truth is a dream. And that only Dream is on the side of the true. How do I know this? I don't know. If I'm not mistaken, one can say that when a man strikes his sword against the forms of terrifying animals coming out from the rolls of the rug or when he wants to embrace children who are no bigger than my pen and are enveloped in paper bags it's because he doesn't realize the state he is in.

– That reminds me of Mr Émile, all the messages he received from the dead in Oran, he set them down on leaves of paper in a very precise order and left them all night in his closet.

– *Aeneas*, I say, not *Émile*.

– They stay as they are and without being disturbed. But early in the morning when the hinges of the door turn, the slight wind of the door, said Mr Émile, weaves my mother, dispersed those leaves, and neither the medium nor his sister was able or tried to catch those oracles so that there was never any proof. When one expects revelations, one leaves without an answer. This *Schwind*, it resembles something that disappears in German, says my mother. Who knows if he didn't mean to paint something that is in his name? *Geschwind*, that's rapid.

That's rapid, says my slow mother, this Mister Rapid is someone who is elsewhere at the same time. His ideas are rapid that's all. Because he doesn't have even a Cent – or a Shoe – to his name, despite his fine white shirt – says my mother whose voice wanders off in a reverie then – I don't know why they are in prison. The Rapids are the ones who take off violently at a higher than average speed in their category and whose course is invariably stopped by the Slows whose average number is far superior to those who do things in little time. Me, I'm a rapid to whom your grandmother used to say why do things quickly when one has the time to go slowly.

There are people who are in prison, they don't even know what has happened to them. Prison is habit.

On Sundays Mr Émile used to go into the prisons

Here I cut the thread. – We're talking about Aeneas, I say. Do you know Aeneas? I say. – Aeneas? It seems to me he's the brother of the wife of Onkel Oskar who didn't die of hunger in Theresienstadt thanks to Omi's sisters-in-law, the sisters of my father.

If there is only one spider in Montaigne's Tower it is because the bats feed on everything that insects the abode. The only one that escapes this fate is the author of the small web hanging in the corner of the grate whose bars are now always on my mind. Since it is extraordinarily tidy and painted in trompe-l'oeil, I had initially taken this figure for a work of real silk, I thought I saw it vibrate very slightly, but it was a vibration of the interior light coming from the window up high to the right that produced this false likeness. I completely forgot about this web whose spider has disappeared as irreparably as the occupants of the jail. Of Pero and Cimon there remains not a trace above the fireplace. In his reveries, Montaigne believed sometimes he was Pero but right away found she resembled the beloved and saw himself reflected in all his ardor and transported into the hallucinated face that Cimon turns toward Pero the way the ecstatic dog takes his master for God.

When I look at the body that is my mother stretched out

on the couch, that is to say the body she offers up to my gaze with a smile unlimited in time, for she smiles, at me, calmly and at length, it's another manner of conversation, I absorb some immaterial and desirable substance that emanates from her and from me, I am but a wide avid soul, a spiritual mouth and tongue, which aspire to pump the vital saps, the teeming visions, the luminous pastures, I graze on everything that is my mother, this economical and neat abundance, I take sustenance from what she is, constant, tenacious, centuries-rich, without bitterness, and I suckle, thinking: once again today I lack for nothing, but tomorrow. Pause

– I ate some turbot, says my mother. She remembers the turbot with fondness. I see the turbot now in her eyes. She still sees this turbot.

– Really beautiful the turbot, says my mother. That the turbot is beautiful is an appreciable plus. And you? I had a turbot: something.

And me too. I receive the beautiful turbot something. She eats for me. I eat her.

– I am replacing, says my mother.

That too I carry to my soul's mouth, but I don't know exactly what taste "I am replacing" has.

– I am lucky to be still-here. So much the better if one is lucky. One doesn't choose one's lot.

Her lot: being-still-here. The lot has a natural logic.

– I am replacing those who have left early. I am replacing my father, I am replacing my husband. And you? What did you eat?

– Some of you. Of your turbot. Some chicken of you.

I can't contemplate you without pulling off leg or breast.

– My presence is a habit, says my mother. She sucks on a piece of chocolate. But one never gets habituated to habit.

How much time still? For how much time? How many more times?

57

Dreams! Specters of speculations!

Speculations often occur to me concerning the length of our lives, if not often at least sometimes. Naturally I chase them away. Thinks my uncle Freud. But not without having first granted them a well-honed hospitality. Thinks my uncle Freud. The idea that my sixty-seventh birthday could be the last did not prove true. The idea that my sixty-eighth birthday could be the last imposed itself both on me and the City of Vienna. No one being sure of tomorrow, the idea of the last birthday has presented itself again every year. Once my birthday is passed I feel cured of the birthday for a while. Besides the idea, the garden is more and more lovely.

Every Sunday I wind up the clock in my study, Freud was saying to himself, once a week I get on the road again, in the end one doesn't know which day will end up the last. You can't imagine the infantile and baleful panic that overtook him on the famous Monday in July 1939 when he brutally discovers that he has forgotten to wind up the clock. There is as yet no one awake in the house. With all imaginable difficulty he tries to "feed" the clock, that's the word that occurs to him. He inserts the key first of all behind the little bed in the study, an absurd gesture. He has to move several times. He doesn't fall, but he is going to fall, or the other way around. He gazes with a desperate look at his dog who has curled up in the most remote corner of the room and gazes at him with a desperate look. Poor dogs, they think. One can stuff oneself with sadness. At that moment, he does not even see the clock anymore, which is still on the mantle of the fireplace, although he sees a clock that resembles it. The whole household begins to wake up. They will see. First the maid quickly sets breakfast on the round table, for life goes on one step away from distress. The sun also arrives through the window, which might wake him up before he has succeeded in winding up the clock. He answers the maid in a non sequitur. The anguish of the end is declared with the words "at that moment" that sharpen the sorrow at not being able to lay his hand on the clock, the idea that it might stop, the painful stupefaction of realizing that he was able to commit such an omission, the internal division this causes him. Soon he had but one thought, one goal. But without any glimmer of interpretation. Wind up. Wind up. Anna was there. The idea of finding himself without this something that had become in such a short time the Signal was intolerable to him. – Anna? After all she knows the layout of the place, she knows her father, her sight is good. Why not ask her to help him? It's as if he lacked faith in Anna, like the clock, a madness, an injustice. He ends by overcoming his inexplicable resistance and asking her for help. Perhaps it was hope to which he couldn't manage to hoist himself up? Anna says: but it's there, on the mantle of the fireplace, as always. Alas! There? It was the famous illusion he had had a little earlier! The false clock. Here he reached Despair. Despair took exactly the place of the clock. It was sitting on the fireplace like a time bomb. Even awake, Freud couldn't manage to get out of Despair. He was tempted to tell Anna about it, but didn't have the strength. Strength had abandoned him. Here I am fallen under the power of the Peau de Chagrin, he said to himself. I cannot prevent myself from foreseeing the end and thus of attracting it. But how to stop reading *La Peau de chagrin*? It is the only book that devours you. Afterward Freud noticed that there were now feelings between him and the clock. Sometimes it was hatred. Naturally it was he who lent it his feelings. It was as if the clock had abandoned him whereas it was he who had forgotten to wind it up. That he believed he had forgotten it made no difference at all. Dream is reality avoided for a time. One doesn't die, thought Freud, one doesn't commit suicide either. A day comes when one forgets not to die. It's due to fatigue.

Peter Paul Rubens, *Cimon and Pero*

THE SHRINKING

No one can describe the pain of shrinking. One can only
suffer it. The Shrinking is a Giant Ghost. No one knows if it
is internal or external. One suffers from the lost Object, from
lost space, one suffers from a fleeting suffering, from lost ills,
from the stuntings of the orifices of memory, from hernias
of the mind's throat, one feels that one has something like
a contraction of the conduits, the temples. It's a matter of a
piece of flesh and skin the size of an invasive notebook. One
has a lostnotebook, that is to say an intolerable feeling of
lostnotebook under the skull, one has lostnotebook in the
skull of forgettings, one has the devil in the box of forgettings, a flabby, fidgety devil who froths at the walls of the
skull, the worst enemy of man which is the diabolical regi-
ment of his own resistances, these little pieces of sticky filth
that are his filth himself, have to find this lostnotebook and
put it back in its place in the head where the hole it makes is
completely filled by hardened hardened devil's skin, corklike
skin, dilatable cork of skin that fills to bursting all the room

for thought. To have the inflatable ghostobject under the vault so that there is no more space to slip in a self is an ache whose color cannot be told and that has no form because it is us. It's a matter of a bone of me become foreign, which being me does not clear out of my head which not being me makes me mad that it is in me, suffered Freud, furious at not finding this notebook in which he must have noted down the most necessary of the evidence of experiences of forgetting of dreams, that which concerned the key dreams, according to the indications of the "Pyramid" notebook, which contained a summary of the analysis of the neurosis of mental starvation if one can give the name neurosis to a psychical phenomenon as devastating as an internal tidal wave: because one engulfs oneself in an enormous swallowing, the tongue being lived as a whale, one can neither swallow nor bring up anything more. The "Pyramid" sketch book referred, page after page, to notebook "S" on which there was the reproduction of a drawing of a Serpent. Well, suffered Freud, the suffering through introjection of the lostobject has such hallucinatory effects that the whole box of forgettings is contaminated and as if counter-animated by ghostly powers, as if by an erasing powder. You cannot keep yourself from searching for the piece of lostme. You are sure never to find it again. You stir up your brain in jungles of doubt. The mental cavity is squatted by an extraordinary python: you can hear it *running* through the head in pieces because it moves two yards of itself in a terrific leap upwards and brings it back down two yards further on in a crash of kettledrums. You can neither give up this doomed exploration nor comfort yourself with an illusion. Yet the certainty that this missing part is still there still alive cannot be pried loose from the soul. Perhaps it wasn't a Serpent, one says to oneself, and yet notebook "T" indeed refers three times to notebook "S." You put your memory down on the table and you can't find it anymore. It's a case of possession by a little part that by being lost becomes much bigger than the whole. You have reached this extremity: you would give a big piece of your life to find "it" again. It's not much, since in fact the whole life is sequestered in this phantom Stomach. Your being has never been so closed up, flattened, cramped, your mind laced up as in a boot. There is witchcraft: here is someone whose famous kingdoms are jammed in a wallet of grainy leather. You bite your own throat with jaws poisoned with the lost object. You rummage non-stop in vain all day, every minute, because you can do nothing other than flounder in the lacuna like a dog in the center of the Ocean. It was white. It was lying down. During the day the missing piece sustains doubt. It was thicker than "T." You are incarcerated in it. Attached. Chained. Perhaps it would be better to stop reading *La Peau de chagrin* in this moment of distress Freud said to himself, but I can't do anything but. It's a book that gets the upper hand. It would have been better not to begin. One does what one fears. I should just stop there one says to oneself when the minute of toolate has passed, at the moment when nothing more exists in the world. That's when you forget the adored wife. If you wanted to call her, not even, merely invoke her, not even invoke her, the evening when she had been a bird you had seen walking on the dike stepping like a seagull, another time, it was very long ago, you saw her in warm colors like a creature from a dream of Baudelaire's, heavy, tinged with crimson, tousled like a hen captive of her brood, with a crest curled with plump black violets like Albertine's wavy hair, you also saw her stretched out like a child with a fixed stare, highly intelligent, whose androgynous smile showed small white porcelain teeth that promised the voluptuous pleasures of a bite, and her ear like a dainty pastry, and the silk stocking knotted around the neck, for laughs one remembers scents some very strong and nights

63

when she was a saint who played hunt-the-slipper and suddenly didn't reappear. The moment you turn your anxious thought toward her, in a sudden fright, you can no longer find her name, that too! lostname? this is what you've come to, in the box of forgetting an oozing fog, you scratch at it, a name in *li* you fear, you believe, Broccoli comes to mind, like a demonic temptation, what a stranger one becomes when one is delivered over to the oubliette, there was some li, some woman who was the milk of yesterday, here's what's left the oblivion of proper names as well everything that was in the "Sphinx" notebook.

What is my wife's name? gnaws the eaten-away remainder of Raphaël, it's something like Broccoli, the starving one terrifies himself, thus one can waste away in the soul still more, the decrease of skin on the bone that thinks is diabolically interminable, it's not Broccoli, but I'm not going to let go of this plank for staying afloat above the abyss, it's in that direction, I feel the influence however, the skull empties like an hourglass, if you found the name of the adored wife, perhaps you would slow the draining? Finally the unhappy man expires exhausted by the fight without having been able to pronounce the word Amen.

"For my comments on a case of Forgetting the name of the dearest person in the world, see the 'Serpent' notebook," I had written, laments Freud. The true reasons why the Serpent escapes him do not give him the least hint. Only false reasons present themselves. And what if in the name of the adored wife, who has disappeared in the self-holocaust, one found a key? Freud does not dare tell Anna that he has forgotten the name of a character in a book that he finished reading less than an hour ago. He has just time enough to take it back from out of her hands, and it's Pauline, something with oli. What if he had been able to call Pauline. The

64

box of forgetting is ruthless. It can be compared to the organ of vengeance.

I have never lost anything, says my mother.

Having gotten to this page everything disappears. I fail to understand what is happening. I have always had a case with batteries for my ears. Since I have been here this case has completely disappeared. – What color is this case? – It was black. But in my memory it is white at the moment. I have never lost anything I come here everything is lost. I see you thinking that I must have left it in the other house, it's not possible, I can't leave the vital case in the other house, my children who count I cannot forget, I have not lost the traces, I have a clear idea of all things, I fail to understand. As soon as I come here, bang, there is an ear that totally disappears. Last time everything that disappeared was never found again.

Obviously a reader is going to think that's it's yourbrother. A reader is going to think that it's yourbook.

Atmyhouse this has never happened to me before.

It only happens here. The Plague: here. Your *peau de chat*: here. I don't understand.

Obviously your friend Mister Freud is going to think that it's me. I look everywhere for the case that is black but that is white, I don't find it. I don't deny that the pages that were in the place of these pages have totally disappeared ever since my mother arrived at this chapter. I don't understand. I suffer from privations, resistances, tangles, extraordinary lack of spacing between the threads, regrets and various pangs.

And the trash? Searched, and for nothing. My brother first, then me.

She is sitting on the edge of her bed, bent at the waist, absorbed, in the attitude of a model who has taken up her pose. I approach. What captivates her are: the batteries. Some round things are grazing on her lap, motionless insects. Did you find them again? No. They were in the case. When I got here the case was grey. Now she checks the battery things. The batteries are sleeping. According to my mother they are bigger. She's been observing them for a while. I fail to understand what is happening. Here, they are bigger. I check: Size 13. They are the same, I say. She sets a big battery next to a small one. It's smaller, says my mother. They are the same, I say. Once I arrive in your book, things scale down. I will have to go into town to check

According to me, there is perhaps some spell.

Her large innocent brown eyes raised toward me: did you know that I had lost them?

Losing is winning: it's my turn. Thursday July 14 I lose the "Panther" notebook. It is the absolute notebook. In the absolute: the whole archive of what I have lost. Lost the inventory of the lost. The notebook remains unfindable. It acquires the incalculable volume of the Extrafindable. It haunts my epics. It lies in wait for me. Is it in space or in time? It has only one Eye, that of Polyphemus. I recognize that it's my eye. I have the notebook with a gouged, suppurating eye. I recognize the interior crater. It becomes a fingernail incarnated in my eye. It's a sequestered Eye. An Eyelos. I am myself under its sequestration. It has hold of this book's wardrobe whose existence it holds hostage. It is deadly. Like every state of self-burial. If one doesn't die of it, when one is en route to psychical incarceration, it's because the tick-tock of the clock is not yet pointing to Death. Yet one is wedged in its throat. At that moment, with a monstrous spasm it writhes and vomits us up, sticky little indigestible insect that I am

66

There are some admirable discoveries, of which one should, truth to tell, be ashamed since one ought to have remarked their necessity and their importance from the beginning and not at the end of thirty or forty years. But secrets are always kept in very nearby places that escape us.

One might think that the answer to the mystery of the Library Closet is very nearby. The door is going to open, a few stairs stand between me and the revelation. This is a truth that creates an illusion. It is a dark forest, a labyrinth of chapters, an overgrown path of dreams by more than one dreamer, which communicates between the lands of the living and the dead. We do not know the names and the plans of the force that pushes us, to which we give in, the desire we obey without knowing what we desire.

Let us return to the orifice crossed with bars that I ended up noticing after some fifty years. How long does one not see, how long before one sees?

There lived the neighbors of Montaigne's heart, those who – La Boétie having passed by the banks of Lethe – were his children his parents his Traveling companions, his characters in the Invitation to Prison and to Freedom, the one in the other, the witnesses of his reckless crossings naked in the flat barge, of the night that flows between the bank of the Dordogne and its foreign shore where the true land of Plenty begins for the one fate has delayed, gentle Hell where he expects to rejoin finally the Friend, to stitch himself securely back onto the cherished one. How long life will have been, on one side, for having been so brief on the other. Bars have grown between these two who felt they were making of their two Lives but one unitive Life, of a mixture so universal so primary that each received from the other his daily birth and every day gave birth to his co-born and this just as naturally sharing the benefits of such a hunger.

One morning when I call the office of Montaigne's castle,

you would see me evoking for the interlocutor the painting that left only a glimpse of what was Hell and thus consequently the thought of paradise, and having verified things, I will learn that here long ago disappeared Mycon and Pero, also called Pero and Cimon according to other stories. I appear astonished and almost disappointed, in vain I question passers-by, everyone has never heard of Cimon and Pero. On Friday my desire to know accepts the situation. But Sunday the day when I am at the point of gnawing at my bones from suffering, when I get up surrounded by a cortège of dreams in the course of which I find myself each time invited to give a lecture and twelve times, after having been questioned by different hosts, in rooms with different layouts, sometimes my lectern in the middle, sometimes in the back to the left sometimes I'm wearing a beige suit, sometimes it's black slacks, I am warned that when my voice goes over the *micro* it is mixed up with every other voice, I never hear and I understand nothing, and finally I sum up and conclude with a single laconic and Pyrrhonic phrase saying: "Of nothing more," which means that I have nothing *more* to say, which is true and which distresses me, it is then, in this state of nothing more that is a real mockery of my thirst for truth, that suddenly the faces of Pero and Cimon come back to me in a spectral florescence. And this pale illumination is surrounded by the aura of a marvelously strange sensation of *alreadyforgotten*. I have alreadylived this terrible pang of *alreadyforgotten* that causes the condemned one to feel all the pain that a mental shipwreck holds in store for one who drowns for a long time while descending eyes open beneath the floor of the water. One goes under, oblivion thickens, the tomb shifts heavily around the brain, one undergoes the horror of being forgotten alive, forgetting seeps in everywhere, invades the place of air the place of light, penetrates into the throat, the chest, one's head still above water suffers, all the rest is swallowed up in the sticky chamber. All of a sudden the drowning one is saved. The event that overturns fate, who would have thought of it. It was always absent from imagination. But, all of a sudden, end of the end. End of hunger? The skin of forgetting is pierced. A breast passes through the mesh of Hell. Suddenly I remember having alreadyseen Pero suckling Mycon or Simon or Cimon. It little matters the name of the father. The name of the father is Myfather for Pero. The scene is real in the extreme, of the sort one sees only in the frank light of dreams where nothing is hidden, where the truth always finds a way to pass its breast between the bars.

Disappeared from the wall on which they lived with Montaigne, sustaining each other.

It's a nondescript Closet: the Closet of Co-existence. This room is full of centuries. I have come seeking the concert of times. Here we live under anachronism. It is not only the sentences that murmur today the way almost five hundred years ago they murmured the broken rhythms of Seneca in Montaigne's ear having traversed without damage the years of wars many times reignited, I also hear the silence of the survivor who has just stopped reading aloud because he has heard, yes, in the still pure dawn, immune from human traffic, yes, the cry of the friend whom he heard no longer, whom he awaited no longer, that little squirrel's whistle, this *oui*, this *oui* with which they used to call each other when alive, yes. And in the silence he has just carved out, standing in the chamber cutting short his reading on the word "remedy," all tense, the word between his teeth, all ears, I in turn hear the melodious cry, brief, recognizable, yes, among all calls, and it is the very Sound of Resurrection. One hears it, it's his Voice, the one that in a sorrowful submission to reality, one had totally given up on. But one does not see it. He is there, one can't deny it, the cry climbs and descends in the bouquet of lindens, one follows it through the branches, one would like to *see* the being, the person, the animal, the friend who has thus just ceased being dead, altogether, one would give the years of the rest of one's life, without counting, to *see* the one whose cry one hears, but that particular miracle is not granted. He is not altogether there but no matter. The one who has departed into the corridors full of ambiguity of the world next door responds with his voice to the voice that calls it up and if the body is not there, the voice enters by the small open window and strikes the air and more than once with its adorable note that has not altered with time. There are so many kinds of reality, and so many secret openings in the walls that we think are mute.

For an old man who has taken his responsibilities, for he knew what he was doing when, despite the prohibition, he made the decision in all lucidity, having all his faculties, to bury his father, well aware that this illegal burial, on the one hand would not lead to the desired burial of his father, on the other hand would cause instead of the burial of his father his own death, which, following his sentence of death, would naturally not be followed by the desired burial, thus a doubly cruel fate, the father without burial place, the son of this father likewise without burial place, who, then, not only was informed about the blow that would automatically strike the father, the son, the son in the father and for the father, but also, and this is where one sees how far the passion for the absolute good beyond good and evil can lead, said the prison guard – a blow, I said, that would strike in the third place his daughter, for Cimon the son is also Cimon the father, and it's the whole genealogy, the whole Cimon family that must pay for the decision made by Cimon, son of the very old father, himself already very aged; one sees here that, with the aim of preserving memory and the chance for posthumous peace for the father, that is, for the eldest of the line, the son Cimon will by his own will have given up the right to the maternal soil in which every man hopes to rest, leaving to his daughter the whole painful legacy of mournings, yawning holes, non-burials and unburials, who, this Pero, both daughter of Cimon son of Cimon and mother of a little Cimon who was seen suckling at the trial, is indeed the daughter of her father (and thus of the father before) for whom she is filled with love,

and since it is in full possession of his faculties, as one may see from the enormity and the extraordinary complication of the consequences of his decision, that Cimon will have done everything in vain to lay his father in the tomb, because he could not do otherwise – says the guard, one cannot deny that this man expects to die. In these conditions he buries himself in advance in his father's corpse. For all these reasons the man should not last long. Being condemned to die of hunger, according to the guard the length of life should not exceed a month, at least if they give him water. In theory, he would not be given water. It would be a death from thirst. The guard's problem is to know whether or not he would be given water The guard is free to decide. The story of what happens in the prison between the guard and the old prisoner remains to be written. The whole problematic of the Host and Guest and of objective and subjective cruelty is contained there. If the jailer gives Cimon water, the hostage might ask himself the question of choice. He could thus want to die either from thirst or from hunger, whether not to drink or to drink. On the one hand it is more painful to die from thirst than from hunger. Death from thirst is brutal, rapid, the multicellular suffering one has is intense. The advantage of a rapid end is also an illusion. The soul wants to die the body does not follow. Whereas death from hunger is a flame that goes out slowly. There is fuel in man. Taking the time to die can have its advantages. Montaigne prefers that it be rapid. Whatever the decision, thinks Cimon, I will be very sad and desperate until the last second of consciousness. Already the body decides that it cannot die of thirst. The suffering of the brain is intolerable, the organs scream out with all their might. The mirage of an anorganic end is pulverized in twenty-four hours. So one will die of hunger. The man drinks so as to die slowly. There is going to be autophagia. The body feeds itself on itself. Cooks itself, eats itself cooked. The brain, the heart, the kidneys, the liver, these noble organs will be nourished as are princely infants by the rest of the body. The man will slowly devour his own muscle mass. He is himself the sacrificer and the sacrificed. Naturally the animal that eats itself is limited in its meals both by itself as consumer and provision, and by the conditions of incarceration. According to some paintings Cimon's upper and lower extremities are tied and chained to the wall of the dungeon. In other paintings, his hands are free. In that case he can devour rats if there are any, eat the mold on the walls. You eat fleas. You eat the flies that once in a while fall through the vent. Spiders, no. For you are wrapped up in the reverie of the web.

– So he will die from the end of fuel.

Meanwhile the daughter is sentenced to the death of her father. She is bound to be divided between life and death that is to say between her baby and her father. It's in the family: from generation to generation one loses the father which entails that one kills the child a little. Nevertheless the factor of sexual difference is not negligible. This scene is full of pride: one feels oneself all the same abandoned by the other whom one has renounced. In the face of death everyone for himself first of all that's natural. There is a moment, in cases of dehydration, when one no longer knows who one is who is dying for what, to the point that one can die of rage and astonishment. I live on the hypothesis that Pero is dying from Cimon dying. And conversely. And altogether the opposite. Cimon, dying from himself and dying from the sorrow bequeathed to Pero, is tempted to un-die himself from this double agony. But how? Just as one sees no more of the drama than a piece of grillwork and the bush growing indifferent to the cruel outbursts of destinies. Just as one reads no more than a few letters right above the door that opens between the Closet and the Liberary floating above the shipwreck of the painted shipwreck. Likewise this whole Closet devours itself, devoted as it is to an interminable losing oneself.

Pero, meanwhile, this is my hypothesis, cannot see herself living very long on Cimondying. Something must be done. She is in the state of Michel de Montaigne standing at the bedside of the young man who is for him all the sweetness and all the milk of his life and who in leaving sentences him to the fatal weaning. Living from now on will be but a dying. Nothing left but to survive, in good health. He can imagine himself surviving only bandaged and nourished, according to the milks and honeys of his friend, thus, from a rescuing book. At the very moment of the farewell, the Apocalypse imprints itself in dream and in Latin on the piece of learned furniture essential to life that his brain hallucinates most urgently.

On her side Pero has the sorrow of seeing herself come to take leave of Cimon. It's a real nightmare. Tomorrow each will go his and her own way.

That last day is a prison, a vault, a factory, an unknown hospital. I have come for the execution, says Pero. Today is the Mad Day of the last time. A vast room. The last right to the last word. The place reeks of sadness but the personnel is compassionate. Pero expects to say immense words. She says almost nothing. Banal things. I have forgotten. I have a red dress, she thinks. I want to gather up each of his words. Cimon speaks at breakneck speed. I decide to take notes in a notebook: "The Romans, you were saying, but I didn't have time, took care of the food for the geese – I note as

73

quickly as I can – you speak of donkeys and mules – a general duty of humanity, wait, wait – I say, you are already at the Agrigentines, it's the serious burial of cherished beasts, like horses, or birds who served as amusement for their children, already you are an Egyptian burying wolves, cats, bears, I think they embalm dogs as well and others, wait I cry for the mares, they won the prize at the races three times, be so kind as to make a cemetery for them hurries Cimon, the ox is old, he has served long, pay attention, I don't have time to say everything." I take down everything, I embrace everything, including the trees that have life in another way, thinks Pero. She is led away. I have the vision of a whole life of burials. Suddenly feverish, I stand up, aren't you still alive? I want to be with you at the last second. How much more time? It's in four minutes, the walling up. My heart no longer lets go of time. She stays. The world, time are led away. Nothingness remains. The worst is to have completely missed the last moment. She was not there. A delay pulled her thoughts in all directions, she did not even see Cimon, she was in a faint, the so precious words rolled in front of her, poor human spirit, she had the red dress in her head, and the socks! she was in socks, the thought of shoes obsessed her, a Vanity pecks at her brain, oh we are nothing, we know nothing, neither how to live nor watch nor keep. She had an accident of absence, a fit of mad weakness. I am a murder, moans her brain. Here is the jailer. He is a simple and profound man like a gardener. He tells me that there were three executions today. He confides in me a miracle: Masculine has just had a baby, right before his execution. I lend an ear. – Masculine, you say? – Yes. He said: and this life will bury this death. The beauty in the terror wrenches my heart. Suddenly I speak into the ear of the jailer. – Sir, I say. – Maurizio. That's his name. Might I see him one last time in secret? When one asks for what is beyond hope, what can one hope for? They saw each other alive in the end. She wonders with that anxiety that throws one into a panic if she wants or does not want to have seen him dead. The answer throws her outside the dream at the very moment the jailer says to her with feeling: follow me.

Cimon is still alive within her. For how long? My mother gets up. I am writing in the Liberary, above her, atop my mother, over her head. I cannot stop writing. Time is shrinking: let me not desire to write more than anything in the world. I disobey my vows. Let me escape from the prison whose walls form an inflexible body for me. My desire is backwards. I dream of going to join Mama and having breakfast with her. Suddenly I get away. I grab the first escape passing by. Now I am pouring hot milk into my mother's cup. – More more! Pour it all! To find an ideal satisfaction she needs the cup to be filled to the brim. The milk spills over a little.

– You give me everything, I exclaim. Do you hear?

I am listening but I don't hear

You are my milk! I cry. She listens.

I am her shadow. (For how long?) I pour her enough milk so that it is her too-much. – Enough! she cries. I am still thinking elsewhere. My mother is a think-here. The milk is that: right here.

What has disappeared from the mantle of the fireplace is the scene called the Limit of Despair. It's about that moment no one would have imagined in which a love that has no name all of a sudden takes command of human events. From one minute to the next the characters are shifted and carried off beyond the commonplace by a force which no one can resist whatever may be his or her role or function. The character of the Father passes into the personality of a baby. The one who was the daughter becomes before the eyes of the entire world the mother of her father and consequently an incarnation of absolute and limitless maternity. The jailer who has just carried the bodies of three condemned ones to a mass grave is struck by a conversion that nothing had led one to expect. There is not one element of the painting that is not excessive, immediately sexualized in appearance and at the same instant carried beyond what has been traditionally reported on the subject of incest. It's a matter of a sublime elevation above the fear of incest. Here Despair stops. Here Life wields the Law over the laws. Despair had been welcomed in. Abruptly the habits of hospitality are broken. No one will ever know who had the idea. It's very simple: it's a matter of doing what no one has ever had the idea of doing. It is revolutionary. The daughter has the idea of taking the old man to her breast. Before her no one had ever thought of it. The jailer asked himself every day how the Old Man had managed to delay the deadline. The idea that the old man might be at the daughter's breast could never have occurred to him. All the same the idea that the daughter could take him to her breast seemed quite natural to her.

According to the story, it is only among the Romans that one could have found such a surprising, admirable example of filial piety. The true piety consists in doing what one cannot do even by traditional piety. It would thus be a case of foreign piety. The story wonders how far filial Piety can *penetrate*. It would make its way by the stinking stairwells beneath the vaults up to the railings and there would insert a breast between the bars and would push the nipple into the parent's mouth.

Montaigne, if he had been a woman, would immediately have thought of taking La Boétie to his breast. But it is La Boétie who was represented in the features of Pero. In the moments when Cimontaigne was abandoning himself to Despair, principally during the dangerous weeks that precede and follow August 18, he dragged his gaunt image before Pero La Boétie. For an old man it is sometimes tiring to suckle, he said to himself. How much more time?

For some commentators this presupposes a love that does not go without saying: wherever there was ambivalence there would not be this nursing. This takes nothing away from the ingeniousness and beauty of Pero's gesture. The solution would have come to her upon seeing her father: it was the first time she saw him in such a diminished state. It was no longer her father. He looked like a beggar. To a dog dying of human barbarity she would have offered her breast. According to my mother, it's a shame to waste good milk. When one has too much, one can extract it and use it for the family.

What was represented on the fireplace was Freud's dream from 1937 called "The Visit of Despair." An equivocal title as fits this dream where one visits despair that visits us and despairs of despairing us. In this dream the old man who has submitted to death quite willingly, he says, emphatic affirmation, the dreamer feels, is fished out of the abyss at the last second. He resembles a grouper half-eaten by the whale. One cannot see his body. Only the large breathless bulging head emerges still living pulled *peinlich* out of nothingness, hauled up by a traction exerted upwards on a hook difficult to see in the darkness. Freud recognizes right away the word *peinlich*. He is marvelously astonished by it. It's the one he used half-seriously half-jokingly in 1900 one of those fateful dates when he had accepted to obey the order of Fliess, his beloved of yesteryear, who enjoined him under *penalty* of death to stop smoking immediately. I consent, he had said to your loving recommendation and starting on October 15, 1900, I will abandon my mortal auto-affection so as to owe my life to you.

I will do this act *peinlich*, he had written, already semi-unconscious but always still a little conscious. *Peinlich* that is to say with great pain, taking all the pains necessary to substitute progressively for my cigar the milk of your sweetest friendship.

The two pictures the dream and the memory are psychical twins separated merely by the years. In the ageless ocean of the night they recall and answer and find each other again with great emotion after a long separation, and they find that they haven't changed much, either of them. In the dream "The Visit of Despair," the head of the Dreamer is painful to see, it is terribly deformed by suffering, one can guess that all the painful penalties to which the unfortunate character is sentenced, the pains of the flesh and the tortures of the soul, are contained in this disfigured ooze. He desires passionately to be dead because he is still lucid enough to remember that a dehydration that doesn't lead very quickly to the end of life would cause definitive cerebral lesions. The head weeps with pain, the jaw hangs loose, the tongue swells. At that moment the inconceivable occurs: as happens only in dreams, a Breast saves him. It is a swollen, juicy breast as large as the moon that lets flow into his maw a quantity of sweetish, somewhat salty milk, creamy, warm, the effect of which is absolutely miraculous: from one minute to the next death withdraws and, everywhere it had planted its serpents, it is replaced instantaneously by life. The old man suckles effortlessly, like breathing

For the duration of the scene, which remains undetermined, he does nothing but that: to be at this breast, drunk. Through his mouth he comes to know an incredible happiness: to cease suffering, to have the anguish of need and to be nourished in peace, to be hungry and to be restored, to be thirsty and to be refreshed to the brims of his eyes.

How quickly life returns and death is already forgotten

like a bad dream. And voluptuous pleasure: not to have to make any effort. It is a transfusion of humanity. He does not labor. He lets himself by revived. "You have fatty substances, sugar, lactose, you have proteins, lactalbumin, lactoglobulin, gamma globulin," he thinks, with a little hesitation. This proves that not only the primitive individual but the physician as well is reawakened.

TALES AND DAYS OF READING

My mother pillages me down to the tiniest bit and it's reciprocal. You should see with what sands I fill my hourglass to the brim, the grains enlarged into diamonds by the imagination that we put in charge of regret. Once Cimon has gone down into the ardently desired cellar, a reverie without body comes to visit him. Already she arranges the new quarters. It is she who sketches on the vault the perfect likeness of a window vent. She gets him to believesee a ray of sun, she brings into the cell atoms of weight: the memory of the dog barking pitifully on the deaf and mute slab that clothes the skeleton of the man he was. And this dog is always himself, the dog that he was, inconsolable for himself. The dog without body is now lying flat beneath the trompe-l'oeil. There is a glass as well, the first goblet, recalled quite deliberately from his very distant childhood. The pomegranate tree enters, not altogether, the most forgotten the most humble of all the trees in his father's garden, the last of the trees, the poor thing, enters by the trompe-l'oeil, with the svelteness of a young girl, and the slender, flowering vision is going to plant itself right in front of the wall, he sees it very upright outside, exterior to death. In the end, all of life hangs on the branch of a pomegranate tree that has survived the storms of forgetting. I go into my mother's bedroom. All wrapped up in her morning deafness she doesn't know that I am standing very close to her, in vain I talk to her back, my voice crosses neither time nor space. She is breathing. All I see of her is the small pink silhouette of her mother's bathrobe topped with a bouquet of white hair. It looks like a reverie. She doesn't move. Time passes. I don't move. I am looking at my mother. She is turned toward the window. At a stop. Halfway there I think that she is thinking or perhaps she sees a vision I don't see. Everything is new. This scene has never before taken place. An immense little thing. She is breathing. Silence. Occupied. Or perhaps, I think, she is praying. She is there and she is not there. This scene could take place in a dream, in a play, in a silent film. A little grief spreads throughout the room. A tiny beginning of future past. I stretched out my arm, I gently grazed the pink shoulder of the person who was my mother motionless in front of me. She turns around. "In German one says: *ein Tattergreis*." With three t's, two in the middle. Smiles. The smile rises slow wide from the roots of goodness. Blooms. – "It's better than nothing." Laughs.

Beginning in this month of July my brother and I sing songs to my mother. This was new.

Voices. This had begun as soon as we arrived at the abode, I was still in the cats' garden. The first time I thought it was my brother. Above my head, in the wisteria to the left. A resonant voice singing to Eve:

– You-don't-want-to-eat-a-hardboiled-egg?
– No.
– You're wrong. You will never find it again.

(Sound of an overturned cup)

Resonant voice: Ooooh! What a messy pig!

Cicada's voice: But-where-is-the-rag-for-the-pigs?

Resonant voice: It-was-a-poor-little-rag-that-I-threw-in-the-ga-arbage!

Cicada's cry: What?! Thown away! woe is me! my rag!
I kept that rag for years!

Resonant voice: We'll go to the supermarket to find a rag
To deal with all of the pigs oooh!

My mother chirped a little laugh.

And then it was my turn, I noticed. The household music has changed this year, I sang. Then it was uncle Freud sitting in the past armchair, beneath the mimosas, who sang softly, with a voice whose wings were broken and fluttering about while struggling in the middle of a cloud of acrid smoke.

– *Nein*, he squeaked, tearing the tattered sounds from the shards of his throat – how crumpled and wounded this voice was and yet firmly led toward the goal by the great Mind. – *Nein, Es gibt kein – größeres Leid* – here a pause, under the weight of the word for sorrow – *als unser kleines Kind* – I heard his suffering and I gathered up these hammered-out syllables· *Nein – Kein – Leid – Kind.* "No greater sorrow/than our little child" I might have thought he was chanting that for an instant. The time it took to evoke "our little child" and the old voice rose up and led his sentence to the endpoint, *dann als unser kleines Kind – sterben zu sehen.*

"What, there is no greater sorrow than to see one's little child die, you say," I thought, "I don't agree," I entered into a long passionate discussion with my uncle, but I said none of it aloud, I saw him so worn down, he had trouble holding up his head, he hummed into his scrap of a beard, I saw he was thinking: I've become a poor devil dispossessed of the greatest good the one you never enjoy until too late and in a contretemps that divine state whose name is youth, today I am as weak as a motherless nurseling, the days weigh on me like millennia and every hour is too short, this year diminishes me, I want to return to port, have repairs done, but I'm afraid of the face the port will make at me, there is no port at my age, when the fatal hour approaches, people grow distant, impossible to remember the dates of birthdays, Mnemosyne abandons me, when were my children born, when did they disappear? And thereupon he says several times, at irregular intervals: "but where is my hat?" which fills me with a deep sadness.

I say nothing. My gaze follows him for a long time, internally, without being surprised at what might look, externally, like anachronism.

To come back to my old personal nurseling: since arriving I have been singing softly to my mother the way up until now I sang only to cats, donkeys, angels, to all the beings whom I telephone with the trusting and immodest exultation of music.

This voice has great qualities of magnetic sweetness, anyone can notice this, when I send it off to convoke creatures who are hiding in recesses inaccessible to my sight, stables, forks of trees, attics, these trusting souls come running, persuaded as they are that they are obeying a charm to which I myself do not have the keys. Myself I am charmed by the reach of this voice: at Montaigne's castle on Wednesday, not seeing anywhere the two donkeys I adore, neither in the high pasture nor in the field, I crouched in front of the iron wire that encloses the domain with an electric current and I called their names several times. It's a cooing. No one can hear you, says my brother. And the donkeys came. If they didn't hear me this way, they heard me otherwise. We watched them run toward us from the depths of the scene with the fervor of dogs. I give them the carrots for mybrother and me. There is some transubstantiation. The mystery of the carrots: through the carrot we are hereby donkeyed. This is my brother. This is my sister.

Carrot-juice looks like my mother. I caress her hair. She rolls on the ground. She looks like my cat. I sing the donkey song to my mother. She rubs her muzzle against my arm.

Here my mother reached the summit. The climb will have lasted several pages. That's a lot for her. She is resting. I look leisurely at her. I could describe the picture in the smallest details. The most striking is the freshness of the light that comes from a source hidden inside. Love is thus a physical phenomenon. Here she is getting ready to make a declaration. – I wanted to tell you, she says, in the morning –

She reflected, I was listening. Then she says: in the morning, in the bathroom, do you take a shower or a bath? Her eyes were sparkling. I saw that all this was important. – A shower, always, I say. – So couldn't we replace that bathtub with a shower stall? This hypothesis transported her. I was precise: – That bathtub is just like a shower stall. – But, says my mother with exaltation, if we destroyed the bathtub and replaced it with a shower tray, we'd gain maybe twenty inches. The idea of gaining inches and minutes, the idea of changing the world, making matter retreat, conquering the past, the idea of ordering water to descend more quickly to the center of the earth, the idea of advancing reason, the good, the idea of desiring new forms, crowned her with stars. I saw her ready to resave Archimedes' principle. The transformation of the bathtub into a shower is a bridge between two kingdoms, it's the mystic backpack it's Mama's Hippogriff.

So, what to say to her? I think about it, under her lamp. I say: I am going to think about it

While waiting, she goes in to take her shower in the

bathtub and my gaze followed her back subdued under the harness of the towels

Here, this month of July, I must acquire for my thinking a new sort of speed, with two aspects: the one supercharged, mad, unleashed, instantly to the stars, ready to hitch up to the surreal transports of the Dream. The other, simultaneous, but slowed to the rhythm of the caution that reads with a lantern. It's because this other life is unknown to me. Yesterday it was shadow. I was going in the dark while trembling I thought I encountered in Mama's bedroom an expressionless woman whose body was rough and stiff, who no longer had any of the fragile and supple charms of her life. To be sure this would happen to me especially in the caverns of dreams, but I came out of them only to fall back in.

I seem to see a star today. But it is so new and unaccustomed. Perhaps I am dreamed by Eve? The star is this distant-smile of my mother so close to my face, which dispenses its flood of moon above my head. This smile, gentle without any inflection of gentleness, remains, shudders finely, makes a lake secretly in a clearing, when one leans over its bank to see, one does not see oneself, this smile saddens and delights me. It's not at me that it smiles, it's at someone who I am supposed to be.

The thousand questions that I want to ask my mother flutter on the landing, and finally fly off, frightened at having wanted to graze the future. Mama, where are you happening, in what glass forest, but perhaps it is a city, do you follow your steps, frail elf called into the childhood of a life whose images and rhythms we do not know? I ask myself. I see her traveling before my eyes without knowing if she knows if I know if she fears if she thinks she sees what, slipping without warning from one country to another, she takes off, I struggle, weighed down by the ghosts of my reticences, so here I belong to good sense and she to madness, through an astounding reversal of the roles that were ours through all the decades when she held the broomstick as I rolled toward extravagance. She opens her mouth, opens wide her eyes, then bursts out laughing. This means: I have just survived. This means: in June I was convinced that was it, for the end of the month. What does that mean? Or else it's a mysterious end that took place in June in the mind of our two minds, and from which we have awakened blooming again otherwise. I don't know which word to use, for here it is the New Life and everything is on the other side. To begin with, my mother has put on little shoes, she has left the kitchen forever without making any speeches, cleanly, saying: now the kitchen, that's you.

My own stupefaction is foreign to me; in the past my mother wanted to stop my fall, now in vain I gallop my thought so as not to lose her, my run away mother, she moves with the velocity of a spider monkey, who thanks to the extraordinary length of her arms and legs can still be here when she is already over there. One thinks that old age causes slowdowns, but not at all. It invents crossways and shortcuts of which the ordinary people we are have no idea. I wanted now to stop Mama, hold her back, close her up, tie her down, make sure she is in the place I assign to her by habit, but I did not have time to recognize what I wanted, everything was going too quickly, I didn't know that I wanted it, it stirred feebly in the dark corners of my mind, I felt merely furtive nervous states, a little dizziness, here and there I stuck a tortoise nose out from my carapace, I ventured a withdrawn glance, I was crushed to catch sight of Mama who looked as if she were furnished with a face that had four pairs of single eyes from which she darted glances at top speed and in different directions at the same time, which explains how she could be for example in the street in Oran in 1939 even as she busied herself on July 7, 2008 with a plate of turbot in Aquitaine, and that she urged on me her Blue Notebook, the fateful one, a day that was left over from last year for me and that for her was happening during the same hour as the turbot.

I cannot say much of those moments whose features are natural in the world where I live at night, but that surpass my checkpointed intelligence when I live by day.

I don't have time, it's my mother who has it.

At least, when I find a brief refuge in a parenthesis, there occurs to me the Idea (and how I owe that goddess who rescues the pitiful word) that my mother, having passed through the decisive gates without any of us able to witness it, is now traveling inside a mythological existence. If these gates are indeed gates, which some say are made of ivory, others of horn, others of percale, or of esparto grass, which no one has ever seen in reality because they don't exist anymore distinctly for us than the lady whom Dante used to make a cloak for truth. And yet these "gates" – or ladies, cloaks, locks – are such that one will one day find oneself indisputably present, thus passed, in the *Next Life*. Some will say that is not what it is, that it is she who is the mistress of the other life, and I do not dismiss this hypothesis, but I am still too new and uncertain to affirm it. I do recognize the "cloak." It is *Schermo* the umbrella which my mother has used for years to hide and show the truth. Sometimes she calls it *Schirm* but rarely, because this dog's name, this name that lets one understand that secretly the umbrella is the dog of her old age, seemed to her a little too readable, at least until recently.

I am learning it: everything is behind the appearance. Well, I let myself be taken in by appearances. In a first period, I think that my mother has a whim. Having overlooked the cloaked truth, I realize that I have totally lost it. Let's get back under the umbrella. That my mother dreams of transforming

88

the bathtub into a shower is perhaps nothing but the cloak of truth.

I think my mother in the shower, on this eleventh hour of a July morning when she begins her life by day, later than common mortals, this lateness of the immortals that from now on puts her out of synch, for she no longer has the energy of dawn risings and she steps up to the action counter hours after I have been there. Here she is at the portico of time of a Monday, on the job: to be still-Eve means finding where to apply the lever that she is to levitate the Universe, in proportion to her possibilities and according to her eternal law: rise! My mother rises. My Mother-Rises. Lifts: the egg timer (until the month of June), the dish tray, the pot lids, the cushions, removes, elevates, relieves: everything. Everything eventually stems from Eve, in the kingdom there are no offices that she does not fill, there is no corner that she does not oversee, the house is her hive, she posts her own edicts since she is the lord and the servants, among which one finds under the window of the bathroom "No Sand in the bathtub," an edict written in part in gothic capital letters in part in crumbling characters that illustrate the deposits of these uncontrollable grains. Such is the force of Eve's law that this sign posted a good thirty years ago has never been challenged in its materiality. It is immutably pasted up a little bit crooked, transgressed, therefore profoundly respected. A dozen or so proclamations follow on the kitchen cupboards. Her voice is written everywhere. A very small-sized spider runs around the scene, powerful dwarf, leaps from one mountain crest to another, fords serious ravines effortlessly, it is silence and agility, pulls an invisible thread over superhuman distances, no one hears it but while crossing my study I feel the tiny trace of these links touch my cheek.

But all this present of Presence is soon no more

I stopped here – because the bell of the Instant rang

Here, Creak, my mother's voice, strikes the air between the floors:

– Pierre, Pierre, where is Pierre?

Pierre, Pierre

I go down quickly. There is some *Lied* and some *Leid* in the air, I surrender to the stray note of Creak. Standing before the rampart the small silhouette raises her head. Emits her spider's cry: Pierre! Pierre! She is so small that I am a giant. The cat at my side is enormous. – Pierre! – Pierre is sleeping, I say. What do you want? – I want to tell him a story he doesn't know.

My mother has three paws on each side, which she uses as wheels and springs. In the front she is equipped with two retractable paws whose arms she deploys, sometimes on both sides at the same time in order to wave them very high in the air, and whose capacity of extension seems limitless, sometimes she maneuvers a single paw that can reach far in front on the ground, feel around, nudge, a living and supple prosthesis, messenger of my mother's body, that acts as a scout.

In vain her two paws feel the void, no Pierre, no Pierre. Tiny distressed figure.

– Pierre Pierre will come. You will tell him. – A story that-he-doesn't know. On the lookout for a story-one-doesn't-know is her task, which wakes her up, raises her from her bed, urges her to accost the passerby whom she must captivate without delay with her story.

No sooner erect on her three pairs of spinnerets, she has to narrate. She is spurred on by need. Already words are rushing onto her lips. As if she was very thirsty to pour them out. She hurries, sleeves rolled up, onto the sentences lips trembling, ready to enter into a feverish contest with the powers whom we sense are preparing to inflict the last silence on us. I have already seen this urgency. It's the one that possesses revenants when they address us during their timed visits. Knowing they

90

are admitted to the visitors' room only for some dregs of time, they explode with impatience, a rage of language rattles them, for every second we steal from them through casualness, feebleness, distraction, criminal lack of intuitive charity, they feel assassinated, they bark with pain, resentment ignites fires in their lungs, they groan out inflamed sighs. List, list! but are you going to listen to me yes or no? And they let out howls of a wild beast pierced in the chest. Thus the father on ephemeral leave could hate the son if he were not the only being he loved. Or else it's the contrary version: often when my father returns, it's too much, too short, too high, too great, so he only shines and radiates, and during all these so brief so profound times that the visit lasts I remain motionless beneath the rays, I do not breathe, I absorb, I unfurl my flesh down to my soul, I am but an eye that is held without blinking in hallucination, as intensely dead as he is

But the race had begun, nothing could hold my mother back any longer, she stubbornly pursues her project, there is no reversing course – I want-to-tell-a-story-that-he-doesn't-know, she says, according to me for the third time, according to her one can't stop the process of giving birth, already the head of the story has crowned – it's a midwife story, one day Pauline met – But why do you so urgently want to tell that story so early in the morning, a very old story, without relevance today, when you totter on a step, with no one to listen to you? – I have to tell it, oscillates my mother. It cannot wait Pauline met a girlfriend. – Come up here, I say, come up. – You know where they went? says my mother. – I don't want to know, I say. – They went to the Negro Village, says my mother. She is holding to the underside of the fabric and she secretes a narrative ribbon in zigzag between the bars so as to wind me forcibly round her bobbin. And the more I struggle the more she hurries. It was a businesswoman who passed her off as the midwife, she weaves with a growing frenzy. And me:

I know this story! – Ah! cried my mother, here's the midwife. And she coughs out a howl of laughter. –Stop, I pleaded. You've told me this story a hundred times. – Ah! It's the midwife! Ah! come in. It was not the midwife it was Pauline! weaves the spider. Here I am tied up. I wriggle. And the over-excited argiope wraps up her insect with her sticky threads. Pooor Pauuline, cries my mother, she was so co-mical. Make room for the midwife! With this sentence she guffaws until she's out of breath. Whereupon with a final burst of energy, I cut the thread. Oh no! I cried. That's enough! Well, to my great surprise, the spider lets go. Ouch! she moans. Ouch! As if I had squeezed her paws in the door. Ouch!! and the poor thing humbly breaks down. What a shame! It was such an interesting story, laments the dismissed storyteller, thread dangling, eyes contrite. – But who am I going to tell it to? she laments. And I'm the one she's asking for advice.

– Pierre is sleeping, and you, you're writing.

Who then will listen to my story?

– Tell it to the cats, I say.

And right away she begins again. – Pauline had a girlfriend, she exclaims. I cut! She repairs. I cry. She weaves. The animal would bribe me by insisting it is not the same story. Pauuline had many girlfriends. List, oh list. This one had diabetes. – Tomorrow, I say. Tonight. – No! Right now. It's a story that comes back to me. And Pierre who's sleeping. I can't tell the cats. I have to tell it to you! – No. – It's so co-mical, I have to tell you. I can't after all kill my mother. It's her or me. It's so co-mical. I remember that one can die of laughter. This idea makes me laugh. My mother laughs. She sobs from laughter. I cry till I weep. We argue over Pauuline. Notpauline! I cry! Pauline! howls my mother. But who am I going to tell this story to? Where is Pierre Pierre? She wails. She shakes the bars. I give her a handkerchief. – There is no one I can tell this to? – No! – Why? – I know it! – She coughs out a laugh.

92

We sit down on a step. She's got this story stuck in her throat. She's suffocating from it. – She had a girlfriend . . . – No! No! I'm suffocating. – This one you don't know, she reassures me, the story about diabetes, do you know that one? One morning they found her in the kitchen on the floor. Do you know what the ambulance did? – I know! – Then pretend you don't know. They picked up the two old women and upsy-daisy both to the hospital. – It occurs to me that this story is starting over in this very moment, I say. – One more one less, says my mother. I have another. Her eyes shine with a childish hope. She asks: –May I? – No! No! No story, I cried. We howl with laughter. An intoxication grabs hold of us jostles us. We fall. During the fall my mother cries: And Pierre Pierre who is sleeping! No one to tell my stories to!

Ah! if only my memory could fall asleep beside the miraculous amnesia of my mother. But I am deprived of this genie's gifts: a virginity that is regenerated at will.

– From the moment I start telling a story, says my mother, it is light. I have just arrived in Oran, the world is incredibly co-mical. In 1935 when I am not telling, it is dark, I no longer recognize the world. You'd think I'm in prison. I don't know what time it is anymore

My mother is saved: in the end I had to swallow spoonfuls of story, I struggled, she certainly felt the vibrations that my gesticulation transmitted to her web. One cannot deny it, contact was established.

– We feed each other, I say.

– That reminds me of the food basket when I was in prison, says my mother. Do you know that one too?

– I am in *The Plague*, says my mother.

That such a thing happens, it's incredible. I am in Oran and I don't recognize Oran in Oran. All those people shut up in Oran city. They can't go out. It doesn't look like Oran.

People can't even go to the beach. They are shut up. They think this can't happen to them. They don't think it has already happened to them. If I had been in there I think I wouldn't have waited until the last minute. It would have been very awkward to be in there. I think it's better to leave right away at the first minute. Once the first minute is gone it's awkward. One has to be a doctor to stay in there. In Oran I was not yet a midwife. To write such a book. My mother stays in the Plague. – You're not obliged to stay, I say. – I don't know if there were people left alive to bury the dead. That woman who is perhaps me has the most terrible illness, says my mother. It's like a diarrhea that seeps out of the whole body and that kills everything it touches. But it also makes one brilliant: one sees everything, one knows everything. I am following it. – Who gave you the Plague? I say. I'm talking about the book. She doesn't know. What I keep thinking about is the *starting-point*, says my mother in English. Oran, it's there that everything happens to her. She gets undressed and on the clothes and the sheets are dangerous stains. She shows me her things, an enormous and very heavy bag, which I am supposed to examine. It's her books. I can't figure out if all the colored mothballs are poison or antidote. Each book, each volume has some. If it's poison, I keep on touching it. On the other hand, I am aware that it confers an extralucidity. It's giftpoison, she says. She has never read Derrida. She says the word mythballs as just one word.

Freud too never read Derrida. As for him, he uses the *Peau de chagrin* as naphthalene. He no longer speaks. He sees everything, he knows everything. I know exactly which questions I would like to ask

THE CANE AND THE PARASOL

She is my dog
My unfraught society, company among the natural
enchantments,
For every watchfulness she is my goose,
She was my angel accountant and my angel secretary
She no longer does the accounts
She no longer files away the checking account statements,
the electricity bills and the tax notices
In the vibrantly colored subfolders on which she always
wrote the chapter titles of her book
In her square handwriting, thus
I deliberated this year about putting into a special piece of
furniture
All these envelopes
By which one will see later the innate magnanimity
The care for the common good, the pure and neat sense of
housekeeping
Which my mother made into another religion

Without ever for this making anyone whatsoever take money or time

She is the author of my nighttime notebooks

Without leaving her bed

She comes to me in the guise of: my grandmother her mother, of the Prisoner on a bicycle, of a little dwarf to come, the bones of all "my life" that I carry in my inseparable briefcase

She doesn't read me

She reads Balzac to please me. This summer she is reading *Light in August* but this *Christmas* seems never to end she reads at the same time several paper plates. When I give her *La Peau de chagrin* to read she doesn't read she thinks there is time and that there isn't time, she reads the PlagueLightinAugustWhereToGoInArcachon,

I wonder if she reads or if she turns the pages or if she rereads always the same pages, finally she reads by the light of her august there are restaurants in every book, restaurants have *fortune-telling books* by the menus one understands what's good and what's bad in what they make, finally one dies either at the end of the book or after the end, in the epilogue.

Little by little I figure out that this summer she will avoid reading a book to the end. She invents for herself an unpublished book that doesn't know death. She reads inside her web, when she senses that it becomes dangerous, for the doctor, which she is, to stay closed up in a city like Oran, no, one can ask people to let themselves *die locked up*, I leave the responsibility to him, she thinks, I cannot bear to be locked up, this is not the only thing I have to read. My daughter gave me this *Father Goriot*. That poor father Goriot was a businessman. In the end he regretted having been so good. That reminds me of the opposite: our cousin Franz, his parents were gamblers who had no heart, with the result that ruined at age thirteen he had to work. After *Father Goriot* I fell even lower. It's *The Plague*. She reads lower and lower. Her yellow t-shirt, her white shorts, things don't grow old, the mottled legs of today, the shorts come from Oran. It surprises me this doctor who didn't think right away of cholera. If there were so many rats that were dying, there must have been some before, naturally, no one noticed them. It gets on my nerves that he didn't think of it right away. It's not going to be fun all these people dying. I'm going to take my shower. I am going to wash away all my sins. The stains that remain I owe to the medicine.

This plague resists? And me too I resist. I am worried about the doctor who is overworked. What an idea to write such a book. To worry so much over nothing at all. I am going to read elsewhere. I haven't finished reading the story of *Christmas*, at the same time I started a story about the rabbi who ate on Yom Kippur, one must be a goodjew to write a book like that, I mix everything up it's interesting, I am not going to read all the time only some rabbi or some Plague, if I'm in Oran then I think of Mr Émile, in the Place d'Armes and his fish heads, next I think of the hundreds of feral cats in Oran who are waiting for their Sunday Messiah on the Promenade de Létang, then Mr Émile and his fish heads arrive, the cats have survived once more, meanwhile what is the doctor doing? Yourfather his health was not good, a cold and he needed a bed sheet, not a handkerchief, no one chooses his lot, but one has to know how to set off *fully cognizant*, when I see that there is no more future I take the first plane, if there is one. I'm reading Marilyn I've almost finished, not much left, there's just dying left, if I were a rabbi in case of trouble on Yom Kippur, I'd make German soup for myself, I'd add pieces of bread, a little cheese, the German sausage I cut in little pieces, there is nothing more complete, I mix. Every day I eat from the plates that my granddaughter's boyfriend gave me. They have withstood longer than the couple. I recommend you imitate unbreakable plates. Reading has an effect after all. I acknowledge that it urges me to feed myself well.

As for her, it's Wilhelm Busch that she tastes tirelessly, sips, sitting on the couch, the enormous orange book, chews, reads, while laughing carefully. Burps. – Mama, is it you who burped? – Burped? No! It's not me, it's Wilhelm Busch. – I would prefer it was you. – If it's me, she says, her nose leaning over the orange volume, I can't admit it. – If it's not you, then it's the cat. – No, it's me. She bursts out laughing. Returns to her reading. For ninety years she has herself been a character in Wilhelm Busch. In Wilhelm Busch, everyone who falls makes one die of laughter. – One dies of rhyming, says my mother. What I love about Wilhelm Busch is the rhyme

Rhyme is like life: you can't go in reverse

I get up every day with one day more

Ich bin Urine

Ich bin ein Ruin

That's all I can do for a ruime

Dank Wilhelm Busch für daß –

What I love about Wilhelm, is the ruin with the knife

I want to see what follows, I await: the Continuation of Events. One time they cut off your ear, one time it's the foot, one time it's the tail, one time the cow from the calf

Sometimes they don't come quickly

But if I'm patient

They always end up arriving

I always await what is arriving

Standing on the next line

I guess at nothing on purpose. The author has to know what he's getting at.

He drags me

From one event to another I am totally surprised

All of a sudden it's death? Well what do you know!

I thought it was the stable
It's not at all what I imagined
The characters of the past who come back without knocking
The grandmother always comes back suddenly
She remembers the boy, perhaps he is hiding
Perhaps in prison. Somewhere always
A prison is hidden. One did nothing wrong
But there's always the acolyte who wants to denounce you
It was the hunchback Maria the Acolyte
In the middle of the road
All of sudden prison. I didn't regret it
We ate very-very well thanks to the full Basket
From Madame Bordello – What is the grandmother going
to say?
About the bars? While the bars
Prevent you from eating, there you are in prison, the
prisoner is you and the jailer too
I always had in me intuitions of life
Whereas in your internal cage it's a condemned hen
I adore him   Wilhelm Busch –
I give you back your Balzac, that Proust who's so miser-
able, Montaigne I don't know, let me laugh
He amuses me with everything, he laughs, he laughs, he
rhymes, Wilhelm is Shakespeare who expires in German
One part child one part adult
As soon as there are hens death is in the back of the train
Another expression that is going to make me think
Hens are not to blame
Lay eggs and die it's bizarre this life
Jeder legt noch schnell ein Ei
Und dann kam der Tod herbei
Quickly you lay. Egg falls. Death.
– Cruel, I say.
   They are hens, says my mother, they were tied up

Clucked and Plucked

What do you expect, it's the rhyme

He has seen life the way it was

They were in good company those hens, they weren't alone

Hanged from the laundry cord

the whole hen family at one blow four necks, no one suffered for the other

I haven't seen in France an author like that.

That reminds me: no one knew there was a grandmother. The boy was called New Year

– *Christmas*, I say.

– I prefer New Year

What do you think of my dress?

During the whole improvisation I didn't take my eyes off her, I had noticed how my mother's outfit was marvelously appropriate for the subject. It was a short, cool dress, a white background printed with ropes and cords, giving the impression of light and childhood, which she had underscored with white tennis shoes and little white socks. The ensemble created a successful illusion of a sort of youth that depends not on age but on the soul. With a sureness of intuition-of-life she had rid herself of every realist concern with propriety, every thought of appearance obeying others' opinions. Thus I had taken good note that she had not thought she needed to hide the large purple swellings that sketched out australias and archipelagos on her legs which the little dress left naked. The knees crowned, the calves imprinted with spots, newly freed by her own internal freedom had become natural again. All one saw was the audacious young girl, one of those daredevil girls who are not afraid of bad weather, whom one meets in the streets by the theater taking off on a bicycle in the role of the androgynous genie of that age of dazzling immortality where one leaps over the abyss, so one believes, the way one crosses a stream, leapfrogging over the hen family, in the manner of those beginners for whom death is still so far away that it has no more consistency than a witty remark.

And this young girl, whom I could easily imagine running through the clearings of *The Jungle Book*, without stopping at the remains of the little feathered creatures executed at daybreak, she had just been hatched that very day by the inexplicable gaiety of my mother. One may wonder if it's the magical reading of Wilhelm Busch that had engendered this explosion of vitalities, if perhaps it was these episodes of violence, these paintings by the death drive that reinvigorated her like a truth potion. Or else if there was in the dress a charm, an exuberance woven from the double threads that, as soon as it was put on, just to see, this morning, had transported her straight to the butchery of Wilhelm Busch. Each one reads his or her book quickly. My mother *Und die Moral von der Geschicht* Freud *La Peau de chagrin* Nothing could have prevented her from reading Wilhelm Busch. The big volume was on the shelves of the staircase. Nothing could have obligated the Freud of the Peau de chagrin to read the Moral of the Story. The singularities of my genius he thought, in the terminal autobiographical state in which he found himself, which is to say my limits, this superprison of my superimpossibilities of what I have on occasion called right away my overdeterminations, have always forbidden me any hilarity in the sciences and letters into which my juvenile ardor would have cast me with all my clothes on, like the black Johan into the pond of Wilhelm Busch. I would have liked to be able to *me tenir les côtés* as one says in French but I had already swallowed the hook of Truth that Mephistopheles dangled before me. Until my final day I will hear him rhyming

Vergebens dass ihr ringsum wissenschaftlich schweift
Ein jeder lernt nur was er lernen kann

101

In vain you whirl the sciences around, says my mother,
One learns only what one can learn.

To each his or her Mephistopheles. I adore this Faust who
plays in the ruins of Goethe, says Freud

Yesterday she was wearing a pair of little cropped pants
in black cotton with white polka dots, fifty years, they
haven't budged. There's the difference with the cats: in the
change of skin. The vital affect is the same. It's the same cel-
ebration of Eating. They appreciate the taste of mother that
elementary life has. But it's something else when it comes to
metamorphoses.

How would she reappear tomorrow? I didn't know. Every
day another. A new arising. The existence of someone that she
was able to be, that she could have been, that she perhaps had
been in a dream already forgotten. But there was also, growing in her heart, a loving care, a farmer-wife's solicitude for
all these creatures enclosed in the wardrobes, and which she
didn't dare admit in public she pitied, these companions that
were very old and of good quality that no one, she thought,
would come to adopt. The horses of the wardrobe the nanny
goats, the bonnets, the sweaters, when she no longer had the
strength to take them out, who is going to take care of them?

But what's to be done to avoid the end of a parasol? It
was so pretty. One's not allowed to mix things up? It's old.
It's like me. It can still be used. It's heading toward tatters.
What a difficult felicity it is to seek in oneself the strength of
a welcoming hospitality for a young parasol. Meanwhile the
daughter thinks with sadness, we will weep the loss of the old
roof, but at least the young parathing will have been blessed by
my mother's choice. One mixes pains with pieces of German
sausage.

She does not read me. She does not make herself a prisoner.

I freely tinker together my barred boxes. Neither interned nor excluded my mother approaches my mousetraps. Scans the face of a book from a distance according to the cat's technique. Tele scopy. A pause. The image on the cover holds her attention: the figure has some soup tureen. Soup? thinks my mother. Cautious. Advances. Adjusts. *"Hemlock."* Spells out: Hem – Retreats. At the right distance, saved, she bursts out laughing. "Hemlock! It's bitter!" she says. My mother laughs. I mount her laughter, I laugh. Hemlock, that is your mother. As soon as there is writing, one can even laugh at what makes us wince. We laugh. The bitterness that is my mother, I'm ready to lick her. I find the burning sensations there welcome

Theme: hemlock soup.

And the parasol? What is one going to do with it? My mother is thinking of the old body, It was holding up. Once it is folded laid down one suddenly notices all the points of wear and tear, the bones pierce through. My mother thinks cemetery, but it's a thought she keeps at the greatest possible distance. There are two rooms that would break her heart if she let them: the kitchen and the cemetery. The antagonistic localities. The two opposite symmetrical caverns. I leave you The Responsibility, says my mother. The coronation and decoration rooms. The kitchen that's you. On one side in the Kitchen I do not replace my mother, I officiate under the surveillance of Allmymother, I am but the priestess of her divinity. I maintain the altar. On the other side the Cemetery that's me. She will never have set foot there. She sees me carrying her to her bed after use. She thinks of the old parasol, I see her leaning over its old thin body. – You are pretty, little thing, I say. – I am the half-measure, says my mother. Pretty and faded. Faded and Deflated. I sense the difference. I make every effort. Each effort costs me.

One would keep old man Parasol. One would keep all the characters that accompany her, the indispensable personnel, the manservants, the lady attendants, her numerous officers among which I would cite in the first place the serving trolley which owes its life to her, for if she had not glued it back together and oiled it so many times, I would have thrown it out long ago. But the serving trolley is my mother's dog. The oilcan. The little round table with two mirrors to which she is more and more attached, in part because she bought it in Paris when my mother and the pretty little round table were youth itself and vigor, modern, sporty, with hair cut flapper-style which accentuated the femininity of a brown-haired golfer, secondly because it can no longer stand up, it vacillates, falls perhaps when no one is looking, gets up again thanks to its nimbleness, and on the tarnished mirrors doubtful like old neglected faces, my mother deposits her various and intimate prostheses, her ears, her teeth, her glasses, so that the little table is added to her existence the way the Closet is the Confidant and Stand-in of the main room in the Liberary. One could constitute an installation titled: Summary of Yourmother. I cannot evoke this monument with my mother. The idea of not keeping is for her an economic aberration. According to me, everything gets lost in the pile. According to her everything can still be used. The citrus-squeezer from Oran is still in the kitchen, it weighs on my mother's conscience with all the weight of its cast iron lever. I admit that it could have a future as a religious accessory.

From afar I observe a veritable mountain of waste. At the summit stands the Cane. The Cane is the event. We have entered the age of the Cane. The Cane arrived on October 22, 2007, I had noted. One lived for years not only without cane, but while declaring oneself against the came. The whole year 2007: against the cane and against the birthday. Once past the birthday that my mother had intimidated, trained, subjugated, relegated – enter the cane. One looks for the connection. The two seem linked by my mother's hostility toward certain parts of herselves perceived as foreign. My mother enters into conflict with the Cane from the first step. She goes to get at the pharmacy in order to reject it. During the whole day of October 23 my mother has the cane on her tongue. Chews, spits out. The poisoned bone. Provokes, belittles, denigrates, sends packing the ordered bone. It's a battle.

It has everything wrong with it, she thinks. Too tall, says my mother. One sees that my mother sees the cane in a bad light. It's not as interesting as my umbrella, says my mother, my cane. All the same it's her cane, but for the worst. Too heavy, strikes my mother. It has a scratch on its head. It's not as pretty as the umbrella. – Try it for a few days, I say. – It looks like a bar, says my mother. This cane is a prison. I see the beautiful and the shabby. On one side my umbrella with its dress, it looks like a kite that's dreaming. Across from it, the Bar. I feel I'm locked up in a bar called cane. – Why not return to the umbrella? I say. It was always a charming companion, a seducer able to play feminine or masculine roles, nonviolent and yet firm, without excess. What did you have against the umbrella? The cane is a dry umbrella. – It's the hour of the cane. The umbrella was a comedy. All of reality is on the side of the cane. I raise the cane and people *know*: they have to give me their seat. Starting in October 2007, I give up the umbrella seat and people have to give me the cane seat.

Eve is very cross with the cane. One asks oneself the question of the cane. The cane has a secret power. My mother must win out over the cane. Once in the cane it is very hard to get out. One must not let anyone think that the cane is the principal character of this scene. Today, October 25, the principal character is the Spinach. I *make* the Spinach says my mother. Then she goes to the hairdresser's, and the cane follows her. The cane disappoints her? Quite the contrary. It's exactly what she expected: a non-umbrella. The cane is a totally naked umbrella. Whereas my mother has an abundant head of hair. It's this nakedness that shocks her. One sees its age. Without veil, without sails. Might this be the end of the Umbrella chapter in her story? Not everything has been said, thinks my mother. October 28 she is still feeling the blow of the cane. As if pummeled, rolled out, folded up in the bar of a dungeon. Little voice. Fatigue. She lifts up her sentences and sets them down with difficulty on the sink. Naked sentences, shirtless, wingless. – Am in the kitchen. I'm making a little chicken. She doesn't say much. We take a meager walk. Without conversation. She doesn't hear what I say. She says: it's bizarre. It's a meager, stiff day. It's raining torrents. One thinks of the umbrella.

On the 29th she comes with her trained cane. The cane now has a signature from Eve: stuck, on the narrow torso of the bar – a strip of adhesive paper. The telephone number. – Yours, says my mother. I will finish out my life with her, I thought. A rough, withdrawn, meager creature, angry to the death I thought, almost as black as if it came from the devil, inflexible, a tough guy, I say to myself and yet one must accept him as a gift from God. A *Heathcliff*. He says almost nothing and it's always the truth. I will finish out my life with him, I say to myself. The cane is from now on a member of the family. It sometimes happens that one of us lets him fall or he lets himself fall from us. The fall produces a heavy, dull, massive noise, foreign to our noises, of the unshakeable. Only my mother does not hear the thud of the checkmate move.

My mother's wardrobe is constantly chattering. You'd think it was a bird cage, a Viennese café

Whereas on my side witnesses observe a silence of sleepers. Innumerable and mislaid are my mother notebooks. They are all called Eve. Eve, Eve, Eve, Eve, I am looking for the point of view of Truth. From the author's point of view, in vain one takes first one path then the opposite path, one never reaches the summit. I get lost in front of my mother, I am overrun, a flock of fears cackles around me *UmGott Gott*, goodgod-goodgod gobbledygook, I dream of cages and trunks full of crappycopybooks. One morning when I spend a lifetime looking for the copybook "Eve Strasbourg," I don't find it, I search, I dig I crater my brains to the bone what's the good of keeping so as not to find, lostlost cackle the condemned ones, a gentleman on the telephone tells me in a low voice that we the living are the dead not yet – the dead not yet? I say – the low voice – the dead not yet entered – as if the gentleman were dictating in my ear what I was just then thinking – yes I say the dead not yet entered, yes, I say to myself and it's all regrettable – let me finish, lower your voice – we are the dead notyet notyetentered upon our functions, says the voice and a wave of coughing swallows it up. *Functionary!* A word that comes from my mother's history. Thus voices read my thoughts beneath the muteness that I drape over my tongue. I feel a little indistinct personage a cougher sitting within me in my Closet on a stool, it's the foundling, the one whom no one claims, a child haunted by hunger, he would drink ink instead of milk and I suddenly feel with respect to him an acute ambivalence like the devil's pitchfork, everything in me rebels at the idea of abandoning him, at the idea of adopting him, with his eyes sunken like the cries of humanity, and I don't even dream of being surprised that The End, for that's what it is, should have the appearance of a little boy. A little column of iron, the metamorphosis of a grievously wounded tiger, everything in its vengeful immobility says: you are going to pay. He does not like me, I do not like him, and we belong to each other like me to myself. I don't tell my mother that I have The End in my Closet. It walks about like a firework in front of me. Where? At liberty, it seems. I observe it with a telescope, stupefied by the simplicity of this existence without impurities.

And in the Cage, Life: the name of dagger thrusts

"Functionary? Never! A French word, a despicable goal for young people who took vitamin pills with breakfast," says my mother.

Dike: if Eve yields a flood of life waste swallows me up. If I had not copied all her lives, nothing would remain, not even ashes. But everything is written. But everything is extinguished. Put down in obscure notebooks. But to reread would be to tear out one's eyes. Everything is regrettable.

The other summers, she used to photocopy my notebooks, done with

Eyes closed

To the secret incommunicable forbidden notebooks

The only being in the world of whom I could ever have requested the service,

Not possible, to look without seeing, with eyes closed,

My eyes closed, copy reproduce clean up,

Duplicate my secrets, duplicate the most unitary thing

Without one's eyes touching the virgin secret, the only being

To whom I could confide to large clean hands the unconfidable body

As if to myself, to duplicate without her interrupting

The pure indivisibility, with eyes closed, the other eyes

Agile and careful to do things such that the copy should be

Scrupulously faithful to the model.

Standing before the photocopier, like the born midwife

Confident and without worry who during her whole career

Full of births never had a dead woman,

Then sitting so as to proceed with her grooming

She doesn't read. (1) She doesn't read me

(2) She doesn't concern herself with what does not concern her.

She busies herself. Adjusts. Curiously. Pure cure
Without any curiosity. It's quite a large miracle
Of careful detachment. She herself does not see how rare it is.

Laborious like great Nature without ulterior motives.

On July 27, 2005, my mother having spent the morning photocopying two notebooks (those of 1995 and 1999), I found on the duplicate she gave me on page 26 an event worthy of admiration. As it had been impossible for her to make a duplicate of satisfactory perfection, because of the technical limits on the one hand of the machine, on the other hand because of the format of the notebook – for I had exceeded a certain day in May – I had used the extension of the page beyond the appointed limit, added a line then another in small letters, and this ultimate line was left out, despite all her efforts, by the machine, which my mother saw when she received the offspring, she added in her writing the phrase, the last line that the machine did not render. Careful, applied, fleshy, with her calm respiration, the phrase, painted in her docile and gently diligent writing said: "I leave the responsibility to you."

I discovered the thing on the evening of July 27. I had a strong reaction: the beauty of the altogether unexpected event and which on that day changed abruptly the image I had formed of a certain and distant destiny of these archives.

I had a strong reaction. Double. In truth two twin, indissociable reactions. "I leave the responsibility to you" this reply to a dialogue was, I recognized it in an instant, from "you," my angel secreted away, my graceful character, the one whose most true-to-life portrait one finds in the essay "On Friendship." I found there once again your great soul dressed in the body of my mother. Ten years had passed. Ten years had ceased. My heart was dazzled. Now my mother was adding her old voice to your voice. The reduplication, served by the infinite innocence of my mother, deepened the indivisible thread of the phrase. Under my eyes the union of the gods and the oracles was happening. Each word turned on its edge while sending out flashes of lightning. In this kind of apocalypse, the medium of the revelation is pulled into a conuptial whirlwind one hears what one sees one sees what one has not yet seen one glimpses in the background the great and noble volumes of philosophy, one is in the aura of knowing what one doesn't know, one is admitted as pupil into the dark and velvety heart of ultratime, which is what comes humanly close to eternity, one understands nothing exactly but that does not discourage the pupil, on the contrary, one is enticed, attracted, cradled, embraced, mysteriously mystified, under the charm, yes, under the magic mantle of charm, in its music. Before, this reply was fitted into a continuity that diluted its brilliance and diverted attention. Now enhanced by the neutral and firm voice of my mother's writing, I saw there the cosignature of a legacy whose future was incalculable. To be sure I knew ever since I had drunk the Legacy of Freud, whose alchemy Derrida had done, that a Legacy [legs] may be multiplied into milks [laits] by a multitude a choir that makes the lé resonate, the note that stitches together all the lays to augment with each other the power of its evocation. But to me such a fated windfall had never happened before.

The Voices said to me: I leave the responsibility to you. I was listening. You leave the responsibility to me, I thought. I had taken this as the very Gift of the demand, a monumental Gift that raises the pupil up to prophetic dignity and terror. It's as if you had been asked to write a Shakespeare play, I say to myself, in reality. One could do that only in dreams. But in reality. All the same as excessive and terrifying as it is,

110

the demand is intoxicating, fear is a great sentiment. – For example, take these milks, they have the taste and the threat of the future. It was as if I was licking Shakespeare's hand. The phrase had grown larger. It rumbled gently like some ghostly thunder. I'm going and I leave the Responsibility to you. I'm dying, answers now. Who is leaving me? Who is leaving me That? The absolute Ghost. And in advance and without knowing anything of anything, I am filled with guilt. It was as if I had been asked, I had said yes, obligatorily, and left blank, not knowing of which legacy I had become the Keeper and the Loser. One cannot avoid a legacy. See my life in this play: it belongs altogether to my mother, nothing will ever let me stop being mydaughter at least in this play. One is born. One doesn't born oneself. And conversely: one has born. My mother had borned me. I would say to her, and to her alone: make an exact copy of my soul. Do this for me as docilely as the future mother makes the child I had sent her off on a sub-mission. Blind yourself. And as a seer then, predict my fate. And the phrase that came out attributed to me as lot *The* Responsibility. Oh! That The! I have been bequeathed THEABSOLUTE. Who will tell me what it is? I now had a phrase that I held onto and that held onto me. The phrase that bequeaths and is bequeathed. You write a little phrase in an amusing dialogue. You noticed nothing. You let it rest for ten years. Until the day when, isolated, written by a mother's hand, it becomes as nebulously fated as one of Albertine's phrases.

But once carefully recopied by my mother, these same words of incalculable weight reappear all dusted with the childish innocence that is the soul of my mother reading. – You leave me everything to keep. You leave me the responsibility of Forgetting. You leave me.

I noted down this event in the "panthers" notebook. It was more than an event. It was a *coup de théâtre* in the play of destiny, which changed the importance and the role of the characters and the secret meaning of the text.

My mother slips
Into the tower where there can be only one soul for two bodies
She straightens up the furniture of the bodies
Without troubling the dreamed-of solitude of the soul
She wants uniquely to make sure that there is everything needed for dinner
So I had noted on July 27, 2005, it was a summer in the present, before the beginning of the imperfect.
She was in the Closet in front of the Photocopier and I didn't see time passing.
"She reglues a white plastic hook on a tile in the kitchen, likewise, she repairs the alarm clock, she tidies, screws things, runs the little vacuum cleaner,
doesn't read
She needs things to work, not to know"
so I noted.
She is my clock. I wind her up every day
In the morning. No sooner wound up the story works. The genre: a story that happens in a distant present and always begins by Thatremindsme. I look at my watch. – Five minutes to go I say. I know your story. – You know it? Then that reminds me of the story of the woman who had too much butter and not enough hearts. – Summarize, I say, I know it.
May I never forget to wind up my mother, I say to myself, knowing that it's precisely what may happen –
There is nothing I fear as much as Inadvertence.
This summer she doesn't make photocopies
She is my old dog Tenderness who throws me a party every morning, to see each other again is a marvel we'll see about

112

tomorrow, mydaughter didyousleepwell she yelps, the formulas are automatic the love in the phial is divine. Something in her newly attaches her to animal humanity which in the past didn't interest her.

When the satisfaction and the pride of the imaginary human royalty have lost something of their natural intensity, what some people call "detachment belonging to old age," one notices with a discreet pleasure how our coming resemblance with animals becomes more pronounced. She would not recognize it without some resistance, but everyone in the house can testify to it, this year my mother not only pairs off especially with the cats or other little dogs and babies, but often she imitates them. – Are you meowing? I say. It's not a metaphor. In the cage there is an imitation of voices, which she tries out, rubs on old cords, a kind of sub-speech or sigh-speech, with which she produces invented sounds.

She is my goose. She doesn't know that I keep company with the seriously ill, I spend half my life in the enemy camp, I make love with the dead and the unknown

I say yes Mama I am going to sleep

While I am courting dangers, I am the child put to sleep in my mother who is taking care of her ride, preferably a bus

My house is the length of Mama's life

What will I do without a roof without my mother for

She no longer cooks

She comes wobbling in to see if the kitchen is still there

She has turned over the kitchen

Now it's you, she says. She goes out.

To be the kitchen is a torment for me. Not that I don't want to cook, to feed my mother

To be in the kitchen in my mother's place is a brutality

of my human condition: I am already in the future place we rehearse today misfortune for tomorrow

I hold my head.

My mother's head sticks through the doorframe.

This head behaves with merciless cruelty toward me. It shows itself without veil, capital monument of the enormity of powerlessness. It is innocent. It exhibits the activity of the Butchery of Time

My mother offers her head. It looks like the head of Cimon

I can't say: hide that head from me. It's a sheep's head cut off from what made for its calm splendor yesterday. Take that head away from me, go back in altogether, I thought. But the bars are inexorable. All that the prisoner condemned to extraction can succeed in doing is to offer his head between the bars of the shrinking

This head kills me. Harasses me with dreams of hecatombs. All the animals that are my mother and the head

The nasty surprise on this January morning is the discovery of the massacre of the animals, whether it be rabbits or cats they are dead, all of them, almost, are dying, workers sweep up the bodies and push them along walls of earth, I look at this with dread and horror for I feel an enormous disgust, what repulses me are the placentas torn from the mothers they are light blue swollen like punctured bladders, there are loads of them, the ground of the country is strewn with some gooey substance, it seems to me that I myself am still moving a little but it is perhaps only an illusion a paw movement caused by the passage of a broom over our still warm heap. This nasty surprise is followed right away by another end of the world. The Clos-Salembier has been found again. The idea of finding oneself with one's brother before the entrance of the childhood garden that one thought one had seen sink beneath the flood that fills the streets of the continent, for us survivors who have nothing left except the remains of feelings, causes us an instant of naïve consolation. I must however venture to say that I found something unexpected there, when at last I decide to telephone my mother: I found to the left and the right of the main path I say, on entering, two yards from the gate, I say, two graves. The two graves of the children. That is to say ours? – I didn't know there were those graves, says my mother.

I don't want to sleep anymore, I only begin to get my strength back at midday, I am getting ready to become a human being again, evening comes, I'm afraid of going back to die

She is my sacred object, my old, naturally slender rosebush

She is the puppet Half-and-Half who acts with sublime art my delights and my fears.

Until when? For how much longer?

We don't know. My mother is realistic, which doesn't prevent phantasms. According to her evaluations she will last three years for sure and with luck. She arrives at this result by weighing internal resources. All the same one can have mixed feelings about this prognosis. On the one hand she is in the best position for taking these measurements because it's she, it's her body, it's her tower and her closet, she follows closely the degradations. On the other hand she is in the worst position, because she is weighing herself, one must allow for the incalculable role of unconscious desires that are themselves a confused mixture of for and against of foragainst of ruses of denials.

Thus one cannot count on the solidity of apparently objective opinion.

I do not forget that three years ago she had calculated she would last three years. Three years is a lot, she had said to me. I am going to try she had said to me. It would be better if you counted up to five I had said in order to have better chances of reaching the three years I had said. I feared that the unconscious idea of a goal, of an arrival point, of a last stop, would entail a drop of energies: you see you are close to the finish line, you hurry the end. To give yourself three years is surely to take every risk of a premature triumph. And then three years for her was distant for me: tomorrow. Three years? In that case I stop everything, I leave my pathways, I stay with my mother, I enter into the convent of Hell, and my mother doesn't know it? No no not three years at least five, I said. In October 2005 I didn't dare say ten years, unfortunately I didn't have what it takes to attempt ten. For a wish to work and produce these effects of reality it must rest on a pedestal of verisimilitude, one has to have probability on one's side. Not that I am not grazed by the idea of ten, by its distant and shimmering smile, I have on occasion let a film be made behind my security door of an imaginary scene, which lasts two or three seconds, a kind of illuminated clip, I see us, in a setting of abundant greenery, both of us in profile, looking into each other's eyes, my mother's are now sparkling, they replace all words with brilliant gazes, we are moved, I see that I am not thinking anything, I am drinking, I am quenching myself my mouth open wide at the triumph of my mother, she is seated on time, she raises her head toward me, we passed one hundred years long ago, I raise my heart toward her eyes, this whole vision lasts a long second, she is strong, in bright colors, the white hair of my mother beneath the eternal white hat, but already, during the second, I don't believe it, I fear the gods, I don't know if there are any gods, but fear of them has a power before which I prefer to yield, I blow out the spark.

– Let's say five, I said, and I slipped over convulsing thoughts an appearance of disaffected calm, for I was entering into the applied world of my mother where the country is governed throughout by a politeness of the calculable. One does not exaggerate. That is useless. With my mother, in her mental Germania, one manages the passions in a spirit of accomplishment, with the taste of satisfaction and not the fleeting pleasures of exaltation.

– Five? I saw that she didn't wish to become indebted. Five trembled, three, that was clear enough, on this July 20. Three, I am going to try. It is a lot.

I realize that it is a doubtful exploit for my mother; I mused. Beginning today, I thought, October 15, 2005, Mama enters into the unknown: no inhabitant of her story has pushed beyond ninety-five years. Here her mother stopped, Omi my grandmother, I thought, it was a difficult stopping, ill-fortuned, an example of waste, a poorly done ending after a race so well run, to falter at the last hurdle, that causes a profound feeling of injustice, and one doesn't have the right to a second try, the way Omi failed the exit exam, I prefer not to think about it, I don't know how far my mother pushes her thought, we don't talk about, we don't think about it.

After October 15, 2005, my mother entered into posterity, she advanced very far into virgin continents, like an emperor destined to be alone far in advance of an army of broken down soldiers, of die-too-soons and unfortunates.

From here on I have three fears for her and therefore for me. I fear the guilt of the survivor. And what if she began suddenly to attack herself, to wonder what she's doing there, when everyone else has left, if she were stung by an uncertainty, one sees the characters of the play fall one after the other, above all one must not think: why not me? It's very difficult. The period in which everyone leaves is like a plague. One wonders every day if one is not going to catch death. It's a deceptive, treacherous idea. To each his or her fate. There is no reason to do the same thing as everyone else.

I fear that she will be persecuted by the Feeling of Solitude. It's the kind of melancholy that darkens the heart of the great precursors. The exultation that the young Freud would have been so happy to feel was confiscated from him by the SS. The human cat needs to be given what he has conquered, a conqueror who is not crowned suffers from headaches, the lack of a crown weighs on the temples, on the sinuses.

When he had the intuition, the secret certitude, of having discovered Peru, where neither his father nor any mortal had even imagined that one could venture, beyond the beyond of the *Anständigkeit*, for one has to flounder about in imaginary swamps, cross the sea of mother, penetrate into the forests where live tribes of incests that know no shame, there was no one in whom to confide while laughing with joy that he had found the sources of the two most universal rivers, and most essential to the life of humanity, Lethe and Milk [*lait*], really found them and all by himself, like a god, without predecessor, at least in the history of the sciences, as if he had become the first man, all of a sudden he missed the enchanted gaze of a mother on his hair. No one to say to him: that's good! How pretty that is! Go ahead, go ahead, my love! She understands nothing, but she guesses, it little matters what, she anoints him with pride.

I am trying to prevent this lack of joy, which can disable the greatest ones and often puts them at the mercy of the first flatterer to arrive, by congratulating my mother each time I think I sense a heroic act. But my efficacy is limited, I am so far behind, without experience, without example in Plutarch, without reference in literature. I see no true century-old characters. Naturally I do not fall prey to the vulgarly realist opinion that every hundred years form equally one hundred years.

I don't know how much a cooking pot weighs for someone who no longer has average strength. Moreover my mother no longer lifts the red casserole. These withdrawals are done in the strictest discretion. No publicity. The-things-she-no-longer-does might pass unnoticed. By contrast I observe every day the energy coefficients that must be deployed to make the body rise from the level of the bedroom up to the level of the bathroom. The climbing is done in a calculated manner. One doesn't reach the panting stage. It is a walk along the side of the mountain of staircases where the well-tempered mountaineer takes a break. A pause. Rather long. Starts off again. All things considered since it takes my mother twenty times longer than me to get to the summit, she will have thus covered a slope twenty times higher or around six hundred yards in order to go from the bedroom to the bathroom. Right here I lend an ear. Hidden behind the shelves in a lookout sharpened by concern and curiosity. She has just stopped. A great silence in the stairwell. During this pause our hero searches his memory for a quotation from Macbeth that says more or less that one must die in harness. He does notice that he thereby seems to identify himself with the tyrant, but every man is worth every other under the magnifying glass of psychoanalysis. The essential thing is to manage to triumph over forgetting so as to remember oneself as master of the quotation. One starts off again.

When one's strength returns, one starts off again. At that moment I show myself to my mother so as to welcome her at the summit. To be sure I was not able to accompany her during the climb. But I fulfill the role of the chorus I celebrate. – Cosmonaut! I say. – Do you have a foot left? asks my heroine. – A foot? Of what? Why? – Because you are working *d'arrache-pied*, she trumpets. In his *Everyday Life*, Freud leaves this *Witz* in French.

To come back to the Fears, which have installed their bed next to mine, among these ills there is the fear that she grows tired of not having a centenarian with whom to establish learned exchanges, on the one hand, and emulations, on the other. Envy, pride, the ancient spirit of rivalry, those goads to action, fade inevitably in the absence of equal adversaries.

119

There are no longer any of one's own kind. Hermann Fliess remains. I fear that Hermann Fliess will pass away. I fear that Hermann will survive. I fear that these fears these two fears have made their bed next to my mother's. Sometimes my mother has no fear and perhaps always. The curfew doesn't scare her. She goes out after midnight in the streets of Algiers at war if she has to attend a childbirth.

For a birth she will always have been ready. When she was little, she loved above all discovering an unknown neighborhood, to which she went by every successive means of transportation, pram, stroller with umbrella, bicycle, train, boat, then marrying a young man who came from a continent totally unvisited by anyone whatsoever in the families, to go by way of marriage to Algeria, then it's widowhood that leads her to Maternity, a sort of airport from which one takes off toward the destinies of many unknown ones. I fear that for lack of travel her empire which was worldwide will shrink. But when I see her still very exhausted face, her eyes avid to see already what they will see tomorrow, that look of seeking everywhere for I know not what new object, it occurs to me that perhaps up there in the inaccessible night she is being born or else she has just been born, she is all stunned by the birthing, at the very dawn, at the beginning of a youth that no one ever told her anything about. She goes from surprise to surprise with herself. If I go down, she surprises herself by going down, as if she were tethered to me by an invisible link. – Where are you going? She asks herself. Seek. Find. – I am doing what your cats do. It's an astonishing thing. Something urges her to follow me. A reaffirmed attachment. It's new. It's very old.

I realize little by little that she has a more animal character than last year, she who used to insist severely on distinguishing herself from the cat, she changes her being as soon as it rains, she rolls up in a ball, the sun comes back, it's yet another unfolding, it's hard for me to follow her. It's as if she were testing Lethe with her paw and pulling it back as quickly as possible. At the end of every nap she sounds the bugle, meows to high heaven. As if a little warrior character in her were announcing a victory to its universe.

ON BOARD THE MAGNOLIA

Three years, that's not long, it's necessary for everything I have to do, says my mother. There are the papers. There is every day something else. There is the mail. There is the Testament The Cemetery that's you, fortunately I have a daughter to do the Cemetery. I also like to busy myself with the flowers more and more, every day I get absorbed in the magnolia

She doesn't know how to-live-for-three-years otherwise than infernally. While she walks to the supermarket come what may, I walk toward death. And it's not walking: I crawl, I slog I wreck every fine day with the anxiety of the bad day. Reality infests me with monstrous figures the list of which is in book VI of the *Aeneid*, for it's always the same repugnant Feelings that haunt us, in the vicinity of the Separation, the same furious ambivalences, the same brawls with poisoned knife against oneself, the same homicides turned quickly around into matricides, teeth for teeth, one bites oneself in remorse, one stabs oneself, when one writes one accuses oneself of abandoning one's mother one rejects the accusation one accuses oneself of rejecting the accusation, one accuses oneself of accusing oneself, one opens, in the flank of the desk of the Library, a mental Closet in which unfold all day long on the one hand scenes of shipwreck, scenes of seduction, on the other hand scenes of redemption, scenes of rescue. The two places communicate through a comfortable opening, the one never loses sight of the other, they are twins, they have like night with day a mixed zone but then they become distinct. One can thus continue to write in the room on the left while one tortures oneself, cuts short and gives oneself over to despair in the Closet on the right

Meanwhile my mother runs through her days like the sun. The cycle regularly gets shorter but slowly and she maintains her ritual, she states the course of things on the telephone, faithful to her lookout post, since feeling that she is charged with carrying out a long campaign she gives an account at every stage: I got up at nine o'clock. I am *geniegelt und gestrickelt*. It's ten o'clock. Now I am going to have breakfast. I still roll the trolley around. I can pull whatever rolls.

Consulting the recordings one notices that after a year the rhythms slowed down, the days are shorter, one goes from twelve waking hours gradually to ten hours. In three years one will have lost two hours of sun. But when it is in the sky it has never been so resplendent.

As for me, at night, I feed on snakes.

During the day my mother restores me to the unbelievable faith.

She said three years three years ago.

In three years how much time? If I compare the length of my life with Eve, namely these seventy years at least that we have passed gently without major quarrels, will it be longer than the four years that were given Montaigne to enjoy with La Boétie? How much time will we live during our last four years? A dream river more turbulent than the Yangtze is made into a little brook by the cock's crow. And conversely. In thought I am continual. If only I could store up the treasure of my mother! Today I have everything. I am bathed in the abundance destined to the unimaginable desiccation. I dispense in handfuls of gold-hours the rich now of which tomorrow I will be shorn and despoiled. Destitution awaits me. Of this teeming sea above within there will remain the narrative beginning like this: there was here a sea mother. I will have forgotten the orange juice at noon. A desert will have buried its monotone silences.

Will I remember the novel sadness that now forms a mist over my latent thoughts when, as I lean over her to caress her hair, if it's toward evening, and as if I had thrown a spiritual switch, she instantly pronounces in a single stroke the following phrase: "you'regoingtosleepmydearest?", invariably, while raising toward me a gaze underscored with pride, because the recitation of this phrase, which seems so right to her, so appropriate, gives her the sense of being altogether in her place in the ceremony of time. For she proffers now automatisms that form a ford over a too wide river. So if I said to her, no no, I am not going to sleep, I am staying with you or else I am going to work, she would worry about a disturbance in the course of correspondences. But I say: yes I am going to sleep, that's right, there is no mistake. I am going to find you wherever I go, let's go, come with me, we will sleep in the same train car. You will sound the hours with your refrains. Will I remember the novel tenderness that resonates now in these little automatons? When will I have forgotten it?

And every evening taking me by the hand she will lead me into the kitchen to reveal her secret: "Look mydaughter how every evening when the whole family has retired, I turn off the extension cord before going to bed having first taken care to turn off the gas." Then after having guided

125

herdaughter toward each of her mysteries, whose common theme is extinction, I will see a pride on her forehead, in the mischievous sparkling of her glasses while she casts an examining gaze on everything. I look and every evening while she leads me tirelessly each time being the first time since in the time where she leads her life into combat there is only one evening, that very evening and the day before the day without tomorrow, and while I walk behind her pleading with myself to keep religiously the aura of this scene titled: my mother keeps watch at my door.

– I adore you, I say. She is wearing bright yellow in the kitchen. Very surprised: – You?? The thing is I didn't cry out, I thought aloud. I repeat, my eyes on the vigorous little woman: I tell you I adore you –

– Oh! I thought you said that I bore you. That surprised me.

We always live a little to one side of life, in the strange vicinity of love.

But already within me lights up the indecisive flickering of the imp of perversity: and what if you were going to forget this as well, this little nothing, this modest moment of greatness where Mama in pajamas could not rest until she had shown you how she always had her internal pilot light lit. I realized that I had to reinforce right away, against the power of my own forgetting, the frail domestic instant with a duplicate borrowed from my library, thus I called on the figure of Anchises so as to venerabilize my mother in the kitchen, so much did I already sense in front of the cupboards my attention weakening, the sight of the dishes on the draining board, the menagerie of products unleashed on the shelves, had a powerfully disruptive effect on my mental capacities. I was saddened to think how much I was remembering today the sixth book of the *Aeneid* and for nothing, as if it was yesterday, whereas if I didn't crown my mother with the four towers that

126

the mother of Berecynthia wears on her head, I risked making the heroine of the kitchen vanish.

So I went to bed promising myself not to lose sight of her during the night and to join her the next morning in person as soon as she rose around ten o'clock. We were lying one above the other, naturally I had the upper bunk. I began to read *The Jungle Book* and not *La Peau de chagrin*. I had more than one interest in this book. The animals in it are living. At least the majority of them. In the lower bunk my mother was no doubt deep into a Buschery of animals, but I didn't think about it. And not the Wild Ass's skin, that was taken from the rump of an onager. Not Freud's Book of the end, but the other book, the first one the one that delighted Freud's youth. I began to read the Book of the bookless. All these characters who don't know how to read or write or speak a human language, pure life. All at once I burst out into bitter sobs. I was sitting next to my mother. I saw right away that she was no longer laughing. The gloomy bunk. She terribly small and weak in reality as if reality had said to me brutally: enough nonsense. We're going home. She was complaining anxiously of pain in her hands and feet. That she complained was the worst, she never complains.

Oh! Books! How much stronger reality is! I was seized with a panic. I was in the train with her. Thus I said to myself it might happen to us in a train? That's not possible. Let's get off, things will go better, I say. The black angel of foreboding right behind me. I will have the greatest difficulty getting her out. No one helps me. There is no one. It's the solitary act, here. I help her, I lift her, I drag her, I have to gather up her things, her jackets, her bags beneath the bunk, her notebooks of bank accounts. There are also the cats that divide me. Should I take the cats off the car first or my mother first, but then I will have to get back on to look for the cats and then leave my mother alone on the deserted platform so I leave my mother on a bunk I take the cats off, I order them to remain sitting by the car, will they obey? hurriedly I get back on. I have to take my things, I don't find them, I am wearing socks, as always in a case of mortal danger I don't have shoes on, I should never part from my shoes, how many times I've run like a madwoman in socks down Sam Beckett avenue. I don't know where my bag is, I look around for it in vain, but the fear of leaving my mother alone makes me give up. I put my mother on my shoulder, no strength to perch her on my shoulders, I get off again quickly without bag and in socks which weakens our future but too bad I can't do anything else. Eve is now slumped like an old Vietnamese woman in the dust of the platform. So I call my daughter with all my strength and, except for the echo, in vain. No response. Instead of a response, images. Images: our life stops here, like a sentence cut off abruptly: *What is it?* I see summer: children calling their mother in the fields and on the beaches. These bird calls are killing me. Oh! to call and be answered! Paradise. Not yet lost. Oh! to call! And that brings a conductor. So it was indeed a train. With Eve on my back, the conductor helps me, takes down a few bags and there it's all of humanity that the train carries off inevitably. She had given birth to gods, hundreds of babies, she had even helped a dog give birth, all of them now are enthroned in hotels. I hold her in my arms today, I caress her head, I sing her a cat song without words that means don't be afraid, we'll get through this. Where are the gods and the hundred grandsons? Where are the hotels? I see only forests. Perhaps the living are hidden in the distant greenery? We wait. – Did you get my cargo out? says my mother. Meanwhile I am panic-stricken. Terror and pain push me brutally out the windows at the moment the dream takes off again at high speed. I am sitting next to my mother. – I'm not the one who coughed, says my mother, it's Wilhelm Busch. – Uncle Freud was there too. In the head car. Near and severe. It's because I was going to talk about my war neuroses. He severely forbade me to do so. He led me to understand that when he was alive, he gave me everything. But now I must content myself with the silence of books. – Do you have a rhyme for conductor? I asked Wilhelm Busch's patient.

– A rhyme? Sublime. – For the conductor, I say.

– The conductor's not a doctor. – How do you spell it? – *D, o, c.* One can also say a drill instructor! – Thanks for the rhyme. – Anytime, says my mother. I'm a mime. That I had such a great daughter I don't know how one does it.

The idea occurs to me that perhaps it is I who am burying her while she is thinking only magnolia, I'm putting her in the files. I have her ninety-eight years filed in my heel like a poison dart through the sock

Let's return to the New Life It has never been so free. The sense of duty does not grow in its prairie. It nibbles magnolia petals. "The kitchen is you." I am the kitchen and the cemetery. It sails toward Evedorado, on board the *Magnolia*

You will see her at dawn sitting at the prow, the Magnolia has raised two heavy sails like slices of whiteness. Eve in ecstasy follows the flight. Something was happening with the Magnolia in the year 2008. Perhaps, I will think, the tree whose mast stands to the right of my mother's balcony was bringing her news of a nameless Continent. Every day two other flowers landed two large doves with strong wings, come to bring her messages. The garden is full of conniving Gods. One cannot deny that we are in the unknown life where metamorphoses happen to things. Something delightful and frightening I felt, my heart tensed up several times a day by a beautiful disquieting surprise. The foreign aura. But for my mother it was natural that everything was extraordinary. I wonder every day which tense I should use in my notes, are we I said to myself or were we already what we would have been, I see everything under the golden film that coats mythological times. Then one day I stumble upon a word in the immensity of a text, an altogether magnolia word, *a* word that takes off with a heavy beating of turtledove wings, from the hollow of a page, as happens by chance when one is not prepared for it – one reads while gliding languidly the way one lets oneself by carried on the back of a river, foliage on leaves and, suddenly, a golden word leaps, rockets above the surface of the murky mirror, suddenly, the golden shaft of a perfectly strange word, strangely perfect, and this word was *Surfisse*. Now, this word procures the same joy for me that my mother receives from the arrival of a magnolia flower dispatched by the moon and even detached from the moon.

That *Surfisse* should come to land on my desk, and in a critical moment when I felt that writing suffered from a timidity and thus I did as well, at the approach of inevitable times and thus inevitably acceptable and for which I was lacking a language that had to be equal to it (that is to say ageless and strictly immediate, strictly private and totally universal)

It was for me a Sign as comforting in distress as, for the threadbare prophet, worn down by the unlivable gap between the mental nutshell of a down-and-out man of the faith and the excess of God's infinity, the visit of a beneficent crow the very day one is getting ready to give up.

That this Surfisse should have loomed up from between the inviolate depths of the prison of *The Prisoner* added still more to the sense of miracle. Around this golden ring (which is what Surfisse was for me) I saw at a glance that it had been a question for someone of being on "the eve of a premature death." Which is exactly my case. And that one had met in the street thanks to a traffic jam, a common circumstance, nothing in particular, the marvel of an absolute smile. The eve of a premature death. And I marveled also around this thing of strange, impossible, natural time called "the eve of a premature death." I was in this page like an awkward traveler determined to make a path through the thickets of heavy, resinous rushes that border the local Acheron, here it is the Eyrtre, while stumbling sometimes in the sands over which ran roots come from time immemorial, I was watching where I put my feet, and I saw that the author (the ingenious parent, a Daedalus, for having had the genius to fabricate flying verbal machines) had said, in the vicinity of Surfisse: "I did not have the time to see it very well, but it was very unlikely that I would overvalue it [*que je le surfisse*]." It seemed to me that he had read my thoughts. What I was suffering from, but what he, the author, did not suffer from, at least so I believe, at this time, was a hesitation to overvalue well. I realize that one must throw oneself into the night without knowing how to swim, one must abandon all judgment, break with hesitation, have the naïve wonderance of a childling, that one must see the dove of magnolia for the first time in the world, which my mother does without thinking about it, and with a requisite voluptuousness, whereas I toil very far beneath the moon. I found in Surfisse something like the support of an intimate friend. Let us exaggerate, I said to myself, nothing will be exaggerated enough for we have arrived at The Eve. It's a kind of dune the color of lights, blonds, silvers, milky shades, these are the times sculpted in preciously laced heights, ornamented stitched with figures of dreams, angels, chimeras, horses and airplanes, everything that is winged but written in the rosy stone of time, a mixture of mountain and cathedral, at the foot of which I would like to be able to spend the rest of my life. The way two doves come and make their nest on the edge of nothingness.

An enthusiasm took hold of her. No sooner risen, she went to greet. There have never been so many of them as this year she would say every morning and every morning it began again to be true. I respect the mystery. How to interpret this? According to my mother, it is *bi-zarre*. Two things are *bi-zarre*: (1) the Magnolia, (2) the unforeseeability of the end of life. There is a strict relation between Magnolia and life as duration. I'm being celebrated thought my mother. Every morning I am up, another flower! I embark. I am so bizarre.

To tear myself away from the desk I uprooted my brain. All muddy, I come in. My mother is given over entirely to Magnolia. Magnolia in my place. My mother is given over entirely to her ravishment. A triumph. The midwife is being celebrated. She repels. I crawl.

In October it was a matter of reaching November.

Eve doesn't want a birthday. It is in one's interest to cause oneself to be forgotten. As the "thing" approaches, one keeps one's distance from calendars, one takes on a distracted air. On the 9th she brings me English books. She doesn't say: I will not go to England anymore.

On the 10th she brings me a little datebook (two and a half inches by four that had belonged to Omi my grandmother her mother in 1961 a magic book without skin, without cover, containing all of Omi, and therefore *moi*. The following days she brings me one after the other the sleeping treasures of her dwelling. It is the Legacy – without commentary. It began by the notebook of recipes from Oran. It is all of Oran. She comes and goes deposits leaves again on the fly comes back. I make room in a piece of white metal furniture. Nest for her leftover eggs.

On the 15th she lands with a moldy twig. André Chénier Poems. Inscribed: to my Eve, to my dream. Édouard, 1931. Who was Édouard? A friend of Otto's – Otto was a friend of Hermann's. Moldy leftovers of refugees' dreams. It is all of escaped Berlin. André Chénier, says my mother, a friend of Otto's, I didn't read it. Do you know it?

On the 16th: "At my house everything breaks. The two

132

little tables. There's a drawer that doesn't close anymore."
Everything is less.

One hears the ivory gate grating on its hinges.

My mother remembers that she still has an oilcan, a *burette*,
for lubricating the great jaws of the horrified house. When
she brings out the word *burette*, she flushes, an air of mystical
gratitude makes her eyes shine, she raises the word like a flask
that contains oil for the night light, "burette," yet another
name of a battle won by her memory. – "Burette," she chants,
do you know this word? – I don't know where it comes from.
She flushes.

She passes, it's nice weather, she doesn't want a party,
she has a little voice, the witness wants to cry, I smile at the
laborer.

She maneuvers in the obscure pass. She follows an instinct.
I observe. I follow her instinct. I imitate her reptations. If she
pauses right away I stop. I notice: she advances in columns.
Here: she Wants. This is not negotiable. There: shedoes-
notwant. She follows advice. Ancestral generations speak to
her. Invisible old people walk by her side. She receives news
of the past and of what is coming. I see it in her manner of
conducting her wishes. Here she walks along a certain river
of which books have told me the name but of which she has
never heard tell. When I call her Cane the Golden Bough, it
pleases her a lot.

– Oh? Why is it golden? Gold interests her. What grows
on it? I think it's some electric foliage, it's used for enchanted
forests. – Enchanted or encumbered? – D'or, says my mother,
you can spell it *dort*. If the bough sleeps it is I. Perhaps ma . . .
gnolias grow on it. She raises the bough. She looks into the
distance, her pupils wide. Watches. Uneasy. – I'm looking.
Oh! There they are. For an unavowable second she thought
the flowers had not come back. They are there: I take the
cane, I push aside a few branches. Saved!

133

Let's avoid the minefield. She presses her lips together. Let's avoid the word.

She invents a non-birthday. The birthday: *honi soit qui y pense*. One doesn't think about it. We go to the dentist. It's a matter of the last Tooth. Long trip. The Tooth. Let's not talk about it. We get out at the Gare de l'Est. She asks me if we are indeed going to the Gare du Nord. She says: *mord*. Mord station. It's only a junction. Est, I say. She gathers her strength and her speed. She thinks: fortunately it's the last climb up the three flights and it's my last tooth. One of them remains: unshakable. She keeps a tooth. In life. Commentary: my general condition is less good. I hear less I see less I have less balance I have already been to the supermarket. I still have one tooth. I don't recognize my neighbor. I have radishes. Above all no birthday. Less long: No birthday. I feel the weight of sentences. My cousin sent me a photo. She is a year younger than me. She is better than me, she sees fine, she hears fine, she can walk with a cane. – And you? – I don't hear well. It's decrepitude. I've gone soft. I don't have any strength. I telephone Hermann Fliess. He is still there. He is a year older than me. He still hears. But he doesn't see anything at all. His wife does nothing but sleep. He doesn't see anything at all. But he still hears. I see everything.

The day before: she surprises everyone. She goes to the hairdresser's alone. The hairdresser is surprised: no more hairdresser she had said. She has an unshakable tooth. All the same, I ought to show myself with my hair done, to life.

The day. She does her chores. She Wants.

She wants: to go see her blind nephew. She goes. Wants: togoseeJeanne in the retirement home. She goes. She responds by letter to the Argentina and Australia cousins: three letters. The letters arrived in 1998. To know if they are still there. She lets them know she is still there. Head and cane. And letters. She thinks better late than never. She

134

puts the ten-year-old letters in the letter drawer. She wipes off her breakfast tray. I don't like to leave things unfinished. She surrenders to nature's verdict: they are faded, I'm pruning the geraniums. Her little voice hobbles along: is it today? Sunday? Ah! It's Sunday. I have cauliflower.

It's "Sunday," so we talk cauliflower. – Do you need cauliflower? – For tomorrow, yes. – What do I do with the cauliflower? Will you take it with you? – Yes. I will take *the* birthday cauliflower with me I say to myself. – So you leave at 4.30 with the cauliflower, says my mother. "I don't know if you know this story, I had a good friend who was impossible and who used to say 'I take my responsibilities, I am ephemeral.'" The word ephemeral strikes me on the shoulder. You have given in to sorrow? asks the grating sibilant voice of the Sibyl. I am rudely startled like the author frightened by the formula big stupid tart! Big stupid tart! Big Stupid Tart! Cauliflower! I exclaimed as if it were the response, the exorcism perhaps. That means I believed that up to Cauliflower I was still conscious, I was still there! I am struggling. To have committed a crime today! But perhaps Cauliflower is also a Big Stupid Tart, and it belongs to the shadows in which I perished, I fell into a crack – alas I don't know – one doesn't notice when one's pocket has been picked. – I didn't know that my stories had the gift of putting you to sleep, says the very old voice which is no longer that of a mortal, her face is a little distraught, she looks to me bigger than my mother, but how little and dried up she is, and become as powerfully frail as my mother. And it is my mother. I hear her chirping. I have come back. I had fallen asleep and she had laughed. – These stories, says my mother. For me, they are always new. Listen. I am ephemeral. If there is one you don't know. You are not *alleswissend*.

The next day: Everything went fine. She slipped between the sleeping jaws of the Gare du Nord. If-I-am-still-here, I will go to the BHV warehouse, I'll buy a little refrigerator, a little microwave. One doesn't know when. It is already the 16th. She advances with small steps in a modest exultation.

On the 18th of the month I took my shower I am dressed, I am warmed, I have my shoes on. Damart the underwear I have always liked, if-I-am-still-here. She is here. It was the last time she said: I took my shower. After that I noted she always used the expression: I am going to purify myself.

On the 19th there was a brutal accentuation of the deafness. I lost hearing of her, or she lost me. We entered into the period of the cry

The first evening I struggled, I sought to pierce through the wall, she laughed, she fled. The second evening my voice threw itself against the cliff in vain. I gave up. I waited for her to speak. Suddenly, I yelled for help: my hand was crawling with black creatures, I was trembling. Tall, gloomy, Eve answered me from the bottom of a distant, departed, indifferent voice. She said to me: – Have a good trip. – But I am not leaving on a trip! I protested: I am not leaving! – Oh. Well, have a good trip! – I have come back, I said. – You can come back. She came back to me slowly. Everything fell back into place. I feared the evenings

One morning in December, I dreamed of an ageless man. He was my age. He was standing beneath the moon of the magnolias. Julien Gracq has died, says the radiovoice he had: refused-the-Goncourt-prize-written-nineteenbooks-LeRivagedesSyrtes-themostfamous. He had. I am weeping within. I blow my nose with a piece of green cloth that I took from literature. The sky a blaze of beauty. The dream's moon is in the sky. Eve arrives. I note that it's Eve, the different one, not my mother. She spent the whole afternoon watching Louis de Funès on television. "I don't know why he died. In my opinion he tired himself out making faces." Eve is 97 years old. 97: Gracq.

Gracq, the moon, de Funès. Eve laughs.

A black Goddess weighs down with her four black paws the corners of my sheet of paper, standing, motionless, under the moon. "She moved in for good," says my mother, "in the spirit of sinceImhereIllstay." The behoover, says my mother. The hoover, that's me. I hoover my carpet

Self-portrait as spider:

I look at myself sleeping half-stretched out beneath my stomach three notebooks, with a paw I feel the body of my mother whom I carry into all my dreams, I touch her forehead, she coughs a little, she is lying on her side in a ruined alley, is she . . .? Not yet entered upon the function. This notyet rots my nights. The nights now stretch until around noon. The days get shorter. I was in the offices of the Cemetery. I was discussing with the executives of the Organization. On the Table a large box. They are the Bones of Omi. If this were a dream Omi would be *moi* or *moi* Omi by anagram. But since it is reality, they are the bones of my grandmother. They had therefore been gathered up. It is a horrible good thing, which I will have duly cooked up. For years the bones were in a lost closet corner, Omi in photos in Eve's display cabinet on one side, Omi in bones sequestered in the suburbs on the other hand. Who can say where the self beginsends, I said, it has to stop somewhere says my mother, I don't think that the Bones think.

The Funeral Banker tells me that the pieces of bones must now be preserved until a chest is freed up. I don't debate anything. This place requires sobriety. Omi is sober, me too. How much? I say. I pay a large deposit. The Banker tells me he doesn't know how long the wait will have to be. Years perhaps. I suspect he is exaggerating. Up to how many? I say. Twenty years? – Twenty thousand says the Fireman. This doesn't surprise me. I don't debate. One doesn't calculate death. I go out. Once outside I say to myself that I should have made him sign a contract with a limit of twenty years. We don't ask for any more than that. But once awake one cannot in any circumstances go back over one's dream.

– One cannot depend, says my mother. To each his lot. If I said three years, I was mistaken, it's already been six years since I said three.

– Look at Cimon I say: first of all he is a prisoner of the idea of his father, of the idea of burial, those bones are an idea that imprison him. Once he's a prisoner, all of a sudden he chooses the opposite, milk, life, childhood. If there had not been the Breast would he have jumped with both feet into his father's tomb? My mother looks at the photo of Cimon. Here's another one who does just what he pleases. He's old now. Before at seventy years old, one died, finished. And once again it's she, the daughter, who has to patch everything up with strings.

If I were a painter, I see the painting. It is titled: "The dream of my mother with magnolias. 97." I show it to you here with what power of intuition the canvas expresses the content of a dominant situation. What it captures is that the escape has to be made through an invisible window situated at the top of a ladder of magnolias, from which pours the luminous flood that illuminates with an almost unreal brilliance the old Pietà face of my mother, in such a mysterious manner that she seems *to come out of* the storms of human life with the freshness of a nymph. The magnolia flowers, three of them, are placed along a diagonal like the gnomes who successively lift the dreaming prisoner toward the blue supertemporal sky. To the left of the painting, my mother is half-raised up as if in slight ascension, she is wearing a white blouse. A white canvas cap is set upon her abundant head of hair the pearly gleam of which underscores the matt finish of the canvas. The future escapee is painted beneath the cupola of an immense parasol of an intense yellow that recalls very precisely the solar yellows of Bonnard. So that my mother is escorted by a multitude of sources of warm light that translate excitement and visually diffuse what is happening spiritually. One of the magnolia flowers, which is off by itself on the branch furthest from the edge of the painting, presents an improbable resemblance with my mother's head. If I am not mistaken.

Painted beneath the cupola there is something like honey-swollen silence that intervals a symphony, golden yellow. You notice a sort of Hosanna imprinted all along the corolla and that repeating the word sun in every language – *Soleil, Sonne, Sol* – forms a circular song around my mother's head. My mother, alone, smiles at the angels that she calls babies. On a white garden chair, the thick orange book is her Wilhelm Busch. In the painting, the title and the name of the author are unreadable but I recognize it. Everything is gold and honey. She doesn't know she is looked at doesn't know herself looking. On the other side of the glass I look at her in silence with all my strength for two thousand years. I hold my breath, as if one could thereby *arrest* a vision on one look: eternity. Two cats sitting on either side of my feet motionless filled with religious mystery take the place of lions. Only a painting, I say to myself, with its creamy depths, its buttery layers of time, can produce in one image two thousand images of this image full of centuries. I am on the other side. Two feet from her. From the other side. As in the hypogeum of a parenthesis. If there were a formula with which to save the eternal. If there were a powder that makes a remnant of beauty unforgettable. It would be necessary to powder everything. The lions too. They are the living effigies of love.

I have lowered our gazes. The painting is underlined with a predella representing the austere ironwork of a balcony.

Suddenly, and at that moment for the first time since I have inhabited the world of metamorphoses, I recognize these bars. I notice that they are the same bars: those of the prison grill that alone have survived the disappearance of the chamber and its guest on the wall of the Closet of Montaigne's Library. They are the very bars of the garden of military Hells in Oran, I wanted to escape, slip between their narrow black jaws, I never escaped from fate, except through the agency of dreams. They are the pencils and the pincers of all my prisons, as of all my books. Just as we are prisoners of our internal nights. I myself erected long ago this enclosure that I never noticed. Now I saw my mother, dreaming of the escape that is the most difficult on earth to pull off successfully, sitting as in a boat stitched up with bars, rising up under the wind, augmented for her elevation with an immense sail of yellow canvas, moving away with the majestic slowness of a great mythological bird from my desk. The two cats raised their symmetrical heads to follow the strange acrobatics with their intuitive eyes. I imagined to myself this flight of my mother's. I saw her continuing on the wing beyond the hedge, reaching the size of a butterfly and disappearing and I saw myself pouring out floods of tears while she continued, I imagined the awful details of her katabasis without me. At that moment my mother cried my name too loud, believing no doubt that I couldn't hear through the glass. – Come here, cried my mother. Look. You see those beautiful flowers up there? I don't know what that plant is, cried my mother. I looked in vain in the direction she pointed to, I saw only the magnolias. I crouched near her. – Which flowers? – The big flowers, there. They look like a white cup. Do you see? I felt stupid and thrown off-balance like Dante in the first canto of the Inferno. She sees something I don't see. – I see only the magnolias I say. – Magnolia! cried my mother! He is very nice. He came to wish me good day. Magnolia! It's bi-zarre.

Thus there has been forgetting of the unforgettable! The forgetting-of-magnolia hits me in the forehead like a stroke of sharp madness. Is it even a forgetting? It's a murder. A misfortune. I shiver. It's not a python that has ingested the word Magnolia I say to myself. Such a brutal forgetting can only be a cobra. I am terrified as if she had just lost my name without even being aware of it.

What a journey we are on. We make our way on other paths. Everything is totally new. Invisible bars mix their impenetrable branches with golden boughs. The body of one of these flowers is lying lifeless on the ground and already changed into the remains of a wild ass's skin. When she is tired, my mother sits on a bench along the Lethe. They are uncomfortable benches. She doesn't linger there. I forget the names of things, says my mother. *Ich bin ein bißchen verkalkt.* I don't know how to translate that. I am on the road to kalkairation.

I clasped her ardently in my arms, I tried to gather up the small body that a bit of shadow was overtaking. I opened wide the Sun, *Sonne, Soleil, Sol, Sole.*

I am an old Wreck. No longer good for anything but excoriating vegetables. I have not forgotten the word ex-cor-iate. So let us ex-cor-iate.

"Another flower," thought my mother. "It's the crowning bouquet," she thought. It's inexplicable. I lose the flower. *It's-the-crowning-bouquet* remains.

The day after the abduction of *Magnolia,* I lost the word *Forsythia.* I was like a madwoman. Like an asthmatic one night who has not had an attack for a year had managed to put fear into a beneficial sleep, is jolted awake, full of nightmares, at four o'clock in the morning by the violent shudders of an attack comparable to a tornado in the bedroom. Great convulsive blows striking the bed, beneath the sheets, an attack, while one was sleeping far away, in Australias and Oceanias.

It is true that, during this journey of such vast ambition, one was constantly thinking: I didn't telephone Mama, when will I come back from this faraway world, when will the day come again when I will be able to speak to her? The urgency of speaking to her and hearing her had finally brought me back to Europe and I flitted about like a mouse in a theater snooping in all the wings in search of a telephone. While I was getting myself painfully worked up I figured out that if by some miracle I found the instrument that would give me back my breath, I would right away lose the memory of my mother's number. I felt forgetfulness coming, that hurricane of nothingness. I was awakened by the panic. Yet another stolen night, and in the sheet the thief had rolled up the key word. And this white racket that fills all the cavities of this murderous silence, eyes, chest, bedroom, everything is brutally emptied, for, it must be said, the ablation produces the strangest sort of uproar, like the gusts of aphasia. There is nothing more painful to perceive than the noise of forgetting. A blank pain of suffocation. That phantom forsythia is my obsession. I know it only too well. It appears each time that a duel is in the offing between winter and resurrection. The very specter of Spring, the one that will not return. I see it, a desperate mutism raises its fog between us. Tell me your name, I plead. And never ever does the phantom tell me its name. It's my *memento mori*. I sought everywhere in *The Psychopathology of Everyday Life* for a little consolation, but in vain. Freud's phantoms are lords that never say a word about pain. If my nuncle does not describe the white pain that burns up the heart in the furnace of the head chest of the Forgetter it's because one cannot describe one's death. It is intolerable, and yet one neither can nor wants to escape it

The word Forsythia never comes back to me alive. It is the name of the moment of my death lived in the midst of life. It is like a decapitation to which one is delivered over alive, as a decapitated decapitatable, witness and patient operated on without anesthesia and without end. The head separated from the body continues to suffer and to desire to remember, to stitch itself up again. A desire that is cause of an inexhaustible suffering that does not die. One does not give up. Cut off, the head runs around after the word. You have to imagine the white flight the red neck without the assistance of the body the word flutters like a butterfly come from hell. It's a letter of warning: on the way to extinction. Add to that the bitter odor of forgetting of the Forgetting. All those narcoleptic flowers that take the word of life away from us at the moment they show us life.

I had to consult the gardener's Guide. It was not the first time. It would be all right if one forgot only once. The spark from the pilot light bends, crawls, gets up again. There is something frightening that could be reassuring: persistence. Forgetting is born again, every year, every morning, sorrow. As if Forgetting hibernated only in order to wake up never forgetting to wake up. The forgetting-of-magnolia is now a worker in the house. His activity is impressive. And along with that he's discreet, politely ironic. The mocking angel who sways in the boughs, above my mother's head. I give her back magnolia, the angel takes it away again, I take it back from the angel. Who will give me back forsythia?

This overexcites me painting the disappearance overexcites me the disappearance of a word, I noted. Nothing incites me as much as this death of letters, death to death, gang, gang, rene, queen,

Each time that I die to a word, that a mordant word bites me with teeth so sharp one doesn't feel the blade or the bit I am invaded by an extraordinarily tumultuous void, I am totally hollowed out at the center of me there is tomb

I think only of the hole in thought
I pray
I wait.
For several days I live pierced.
I desire. Pure pure desire. Mystical experience: like the absolute absence of God. ABsence remains

ABSENSE. A madness. Blankgod. Where was the word irradiation of god fired to white heat.

I BECOME A CEMETERY
CITIZEN

The immediate danger of the birthday having passed life resumed more beautiful than ever. She becomes younger. She is delighted with the trick she has played. She sparkles. Her hair spreads out in rays of white hard light all around her head. On February 9 she writes several letters. She signs: Eve 97 years old. Or the old Eve. Several times: Eve Uralt. And Madame Cacochyme. She is lit up from within. She rhymes. It's funny the way we wish as fish/ to keep going ahead/ without any dread. Fish, she says, is for the rhyme. She bursts out laughing. She rhymes her rhyme with Cacochyme. I am Madame Cacochyme, the old lady who rhymes. She telephones Hermann. He is still there. That's better. To become residents in Uraltitude, says my mother, you would rather all the same that there be two of you, even if one is deaf, the other is blind, because each in his or her distant neighborhood, both are readers of Wilhelm Busch. We know everything about slitting the throats of old feathered creatures

On February 10: she Wants. TogoseeJeanne. Wants. Wait
a week, I say. She thinks: "Waiting, waiting. Who knows
what happens." Wants. Goes. Comes back. Two taxis, she
says. At our age we really can't wait. Each day one day less.
I get up each day with one day more. One can't put on the
brakes. I can't back up. *Dank Gott für das.*

On February 10 at the dermatologist's. The two of us sitting on the couch. Waiting waiting. My mother calculates.
Skin is not eternal. There is still a little left. That's better than
nothing. We don't talk: we can't yell in the waiting room.
She consults for a long time a minuscule map of Paris. The
consultation lasts a half-hour. Paris is the size of her hand.
She holds the city in her hand. Under her hand. I wonder
what she is doing. She takes out a little piece of paper the size
of her long and wide index finger. A little pen. She writes for
a long time traces a formula studiously. I look at my watch:
ten minutes. I read the piece of paper. It must be a magic
formula. Étoile-Charles de Gaulle-Grand Palais. It's the
itinerary of the general staff for the return maneuver. Spelled
out. As if she guessed that her power of command was exerted
more forcefully if she transmitted her will to each letter. One
must cross Paris in as straight a line as possible. Madame
Cachochyme does not let go of the steering wheel. We leave.
She is unsteady. Says: time is made of skin. I don't waste it.

February 11, it was *The Hour*. She arrived dressed as Hour
with her chariot, and her cane. On this day it's the turn of
her old fake panther fur to have an outing. All the old animals of the ark are taken out one by one. As she's leaving she
pulled an envelope out of her bag. She handed it to me. "The
Cemetery, that's you." She goes out. Fake old woman fake
panther skin. Free. Old jungle book. Leaves again with her
fake skin and her bough. – I am going to go into this hostile
world where I've seen the animals that devour each other.
The worst is the Python. There's nothing to be done. Only

the cow doesn't eat anyone. There is no cow in this Book. I eat nobody, I remain anonymous.

As of that day I became a cemetery citizen.

All my life – I see this today, as I noted in the panther notebook – I had made a detour so as to get far away from cemeteries, hold them at a distance, never to think about them or else as little as possible, having noticed the extreme horror I felt for these places since the day my father moved in there, in a little apartment, I had soon detected in the very excess of this horror an insidious manner of being inhabited by the cemetery-thought, in full daylight I thought about them *in order* to avoid them, there is always one lying in wait, entire neighborhoods of cities are veritable giant pythons metamorphosed into funeral monuments, I dreamed of a city without cemetery if not of a life without cemetery, these parking lots have always overcome me with sacred horror, it's my secret, my flaw, I noted, I never spoke about it to anyone, at least in the waking world, since nighttime very often found me going through the catacombs, I must have explored hundreds of them, perhaps thousands, the whole world in truth thinks of nothing else but burying, I was received yesterday by a young couple, lovers, still children, but predestined already thrown into the furnace, flaming with passion, with whom I felt in sympathy, who live in the castle of Wuthering Heights, right away I loved their ardor, *the first thing* the heroine did was to lead me to a large window from which one glimpsed the most noble of landscapes, hills on which rose a structure in the form of a bell tower and all these heights lifted up by an exaltation at which point the young woman lover said to me in joyful tones: – That's where – she pointed to the distant foot of the tower – I will be buried. I was born here and here I will be buried. Her jubilation cast a shadow over me and I said very curtly: – But I was not *born* here. And I left. The manner in which the Cemetery surprises you is

147

as abrupt as the death of Bergotte. One can't protect oneself at all. It's hard to believe. It happens to you when you are absorbed in the problem, which is insoluble, of the heaviness of the chains – invisible and thus all the heavier – that restrain the aforementioned woman prisoner: how does one make a heavy chain appear light? Everything is imagination. One worries oneself sick, gnaws at dreams, shakes the bonds to free oneself to the point of producing an excess of knots, one gets entangled, one no longer finds the keys for breaking free, one suffers from forgetting the word "evasion," one remembers having made the plan to have a yacht, it was a false plan, a simulacrum of purchase of a means of flight – enter a cemetery.

Enter a cemetery. It was thus already there? It's unbelievable. Right in the middle of the monologue. Right in the middle of the salon. One pushes back one's chair and one finds oneself sitting in the alley of the cemetery, Bergotte is being buried. Finally, these past few days when one thought one was shaking off the chains of a still living prisoner, what was one doing? One was burying Bergotte. How not to bury? One strikes the world down, writes the Book of Resurrections, erects cathedrals, lifts cities onto two columns of gray and pink granite that bear on their capitals one the lion of St Mark, the other St Theodore treading on the python, one has eyes only for the beautiful faces of our mother that come to us wearing eternal youth and, when no one is expecting it, at a street corner, at the bottom of a ladder of lines: hole. The way one stumbles on the death of Bergotte that very day, and not the day before as the newspapers say, as if one couldn't die that very day, right here, this very instant, and right away it's already the cemetery. The manner in which one chases away whoever makes the mistake of being dead. Out, bone!

All my life, I had thought I struggled against cemeteries and the cemetery-spirit, the closet-spirit, the spirit of secret

148

dungeons, but one can't struggle for the other, or die or break the chains for the other – and for the liberation of the dead, but all my efforts would barely suffice to free my father by freeing his body held prisoner by the cemetery, and for the moment I had only just undertaken to get my grandmother out of the lost-and-found where she had been vegetating for decades. It's an empire without emperor, the cemetery-world, one never knows whom to address in order to visit a prisoner, there is no one in the country which the empire nevertheless surrounds by high walls, no one escapes, very severely high walls, but no one lodges a complaint, neither you nor I have importance any longer, they know how to make us realize this, no one knows why they keep us under surveillance, all these bones in the same basket, and no one remembers the law ordering such a set-up.

And that day, just as – and I verify this in the panther-notebook, that day of fake fur when my mother wants absolutely to go to the BHV with my brother, just as she is leaving, taking I hope the direction of the department store – Bergotte dies, likewise enters the Cemetery. My mother leaves it to me and she takes off down the avenue letting out little cries. Bergotte saved. Metamorphosed. One thought the squirrel dead? Not at all. The Squirrel has come back. I made a note of the news in the notebook: it's a day of news. In the first place my mother gives me *the address*. Right after that or perhaps at the same moment, thus forming forever a figure of destiny by linking in the same scene these two extraordinary events, the Squirrel came back from the land of the departed. Just as suddenly as he disappeared: returned. Only that day I noted, *after*. *After the abyss*. There had been the abyss. Wide borderless abyss. In place of Life, in the middle of the road, like a death of Bergotte, like a hole in the chest, like the ablation of an eye, like once again the death penalty, abruptly, there had been the necrosis of the Squirrel, during our sleep.

We are sleeping. During our sleep the Squirrel is removed from us, not the way they remove one of our ribs to raise it up beside us, but the way a butcher cuts out our lung. Upon waking one looks for it everywhere, for a long time, weeks, one drags around with this enormous wound, and naturally it is a widowhood without consolation. We cultivated this cavity. No burial, never! We don't renounce our heart, we don't replace our lung. We keep the Squirrel, internally. We don't understand this act of aggression, it would be a weakness to understand it, we keep the silence of the faithful about this abduction. We do not forget.

It's bi-zarre says my mother there are events without explanation.

It was the day before the anniversary of the abduction of my father. I alone remembered my mother went to the BHV at the wheel of her powerful innocence. But that we should have received precisely that day a notice from the Cemetery proves nothing.

Thus the Cemetery had written a letter. We had an address in the future. And the Squirrel came back. It is the greatest of surprises: to receive a letter from the eternal future. The present is turned upside down by it. *To know where* the future awaits us is an experience without example. I would never have thought that it could happen to us. It is as if years in advance, in a gesture of incommensurable hospitality, one brought someone who in the future will be condemned to death to visit his last cell. He finds a certain comfort there. One sees oneself seeing what one will not see.

The end of the world lives on Quinet boulevard. If I stayed there on that day, it is because I sought to settle our cemetery matters as quickly as possible. One cannot remain in death for long being alive. I no longer recall when and where

I had crossed the Acheron. I recognized nothing of what I had seen in books, I went from room to room in a formless, centerless abode, not one shadow to meet us. What was most remarkable in these barely inhabited places was the visit of the Lion. Just at the moment when I was trying to sleep, sitting on the edge of a path he entered into the square space, enormous living creature like a big restless cat. That one, I said to myself, I know him somewhat, figuratively, but all the same to see here in reality the Lion of Lost Time, where I expected great departed poets or my schoolmates, I was not at all prepared for that and I confessed that I was afraid. It was perhaps Love (the Lord, the King, the strongest of animal spirits – except for the Python Forgetting), but it was all the same a lion. This unique apparition in this desert let me know clearly what kind of furies rock us when we form bonds with adored beings. This cemetery is off to a good start, I said to myself. And then I remembered that one mustn't be afraid it's this weakness and this misunderstanding that make them violent. So I calmed myself down, and him too, by scratching his head, I gave him satisfaction. Later, when I was crossing through the vast white-tiled rooms and still totally devoid of future, with the lion by my side, there was all the same a bit of rumpus: there was a patch of ground where some hens were pecking. They had red and white feathers and were very round. Being real hens, they were terrified by the lion. No doubt he was contemplating pouncing on them. One hen started screaming and running to escape him. The lion roared. I was on the side of that hen. Not that I loved the lion less. But I can't not be on the side of the devourable ones. In the face of the python, I am entirely with the lion. In this case I was heartsick for her. What to do to save her? I tapped on the lion's nose. The hen was screeching. The idea of a murder will always be unbearable to me. It seems to me that I'm the one who commits it. And yet, I said to myself, what was I doing here, visiting the posthumous world? I realized that I was seeking, on these deserted shelves, the last book. I was very eager to know if it had already been written, what it would be, who it would remember in the end. But I did not find it, on Quinet boulevard.

– Quinet, says my mother, you can spell that *qui naît* and also *qui n'est*. She thinks about rhyming, I see us already under the fog of hallucination lying together, there, with a lion and a hen by our sides. – I am burying myself with Mama, I say. I hear my mother's very small voice crackle like a field mouse in the telephone. Hello? Should I make some beans? – Make beans, mother. We will climb on the ropes of their stalks from the cellar up to the yellow air that pours its living gold through my basement window. – The cemetery, what a future! says my mother. It's funny, man, this creation, how odd that sometimes it's buried god-knows-where, like your-father that reminds me my ears that someone threw away, they've disappeared into the trash, it's really unbelievable.

Life that is being born

Since the sky was low and heavy, I was beneath the cover in what a state I was my god that New Year's night in the Jewish-cemetery: it's a garage, in which I found all the way in the back – thus, among the first to be buried – of the story, of my life, the tomb of my father. I was suffering from those paralyses that overtake me as soon as I enter into the chamber of a dream. The goal is to go where my father is waiting for me. A part of me, from the head to the waist, tries, reaches out, but my legs don't follow, I have to take them in my hands, lift up the inert branches with my hands, an exercise in powerlessness, hoping and in vain that a passerby will agree to drag me half-corpse that I am, but not one passerby, if it's not an attack of this paralysis that will end up carrying me off, having warned me so many times in the past, for this is but a rehearsal of what awaits me at the exit, then it is as was the case this night great dagger blows of illness, whose message is the same: stop, don't continue, don't take a step. And it was with a supreme wrenching that I had – it was necessary – found papa again. He, the poor man, the beloved man, could not come to me naturally, it is the dead-not-yet-entered-upon-their-function like me who must *make* the trip. One cannot crawl in the earth except at the price of these awful gesticulations. It was dark and warm, everything was said, I got breath back from my father and it was Sunday we were alone in the cellar, I thought I was at home, but on Monday, there was a crowd, while I was stretched out on the tomb's couch, writing in the darkness, all these Jews who were talking to me, asking me questions and since I didn't answer taking me for a foreigner they spoke to me in English. No privacy. One mustn't come during the week, I said to myself, only on Sunday. Whereupon at dawn I was ready to leave, in a still worse reality than the false reality of the night, I could no longer stop myself going from one cemetery to another in dream in reality, I couldn't stay, either in dream or in reality. I fell out of bed without delay, leaving behind me my father's garage. I ate three potatoes. I was obligated. I am bergotting, I said to myself. Or else I am going into the Aeneid. I had been told that the tablet of Baudelaire's tomb was now strewn with pebbles, although he was not Jewish and with bits of paper in various colors. I ran before daylight to the Cemetery that is open only after 9 o'clock. I was powerless to do anything else. It is naturally absurd to run hours in advance, present oneself before the closed gates, one doesn't see the urgency but one obeys it. One is alone. One has always been early. As if one wanted to be sure not to miss death. To be the first to enter.

The lady from the agency took me on a visit. She was a very pale lady whose name was Leterme and she didn't say a word. Me too, the anguished shadow that I was, I had nothing to say. I followed, I felt suddenly dizzy, I didn't walk, I floated,

I passed in front of Baudelaire's grave without seeing it, since the low and heavy sky was weighing on me like a cover I couldn't see two yards in front of me, with what nostalgia I remembered the cascade of light that crossed the shadows of the prisoner's brain. As for me, I was walking doubled over dragging my body with my feet beneath streaks of rain that sketched out in front of me imitations of bars. At the back there was a wall. It was the wall of the world. Everything here was stone and bone and I was the vanishing of myself. I had a distant thought for my mother who was living. A few graves further, Leterme, the agent, pointed out with a forefinger the place where all the books stop. One should never have seen that. It is incurable. When Freud saw his naked bone in the mirror he passed without a word through the hole in his jaw to the other side. Others tried to immerse him in an atmosphere of optimism by telling him that the shrinking of the wild ass's skin was going to regress in the opposite direction. To be sure, one will have still other adventures before nightfall, but nothing can change the fact of seeing the hole. I saw in the mirror the hole that my mother made in my cheek while passing to the other side.

I call Eve all the same. She yells: is it accessible? My mother yells because she cannot hear. She thinks it's I who am deaf. And in truth, the mute, the deaf one is me. And it's as if I had heard the lovely call of the lark. These heavenly little persons make their nest in the ground and rise up all at once, pure song, toward the heights, so that one has the marvelous impression that the earth is whistling. – Accessible? my mother was yelling. – Perfectly, I said. You go down a little step, you turn to the right-hand side right away, and it's three yards further on, I say.

– Not too many big crosses? yells my mother. I vaguely weigh too many and big: where do too many and big begin? I don't want to immerse her in a false optimism. So I say: that's all there is. But in front of us, I say, in truth, simple, rusted, nothing.

– I just read an article, says my mother, there are creatures that never die. They are single-celled. But man, since he was given the possibility of reproducing himself, so I have to do my burial. The necessary must be done for the coffin and the formalities.

The papers are her, the hole is me.

– Man, says my mother. What a perspective. The man who escaped from the chain gang of Jews, do you know that one? Why should I stay chained up in this chain gang? he said to himself. He escapes, he hides. He made imaginary condoms. I had gone to see him in Brussels. There was marriage as an ulterior motive. Whatever are imaginary condoms? – Condoms with the heads of bearded men I don't know if there was one or several heads.

The postcard from Hete, you know that? Omi's older sister. Without stamp that she threw out of the window of the train: I don't know where they are taking us. She survived, her husband died there, at Theresien I think, she came back, she lived in the USA with her daughter for two more years she died of a cancer of the eye.

On April 19 she gives her version of Passover: the exodus from Egypt the crossing of the Jordin she says. It's a version without Moses. Then the desert: God says these Old People one has to get rid of them. They have picked up bad habits. There's nothing to be done. They make idols. They make a calf that they adore. Only the young ones can return to the promised Land. In the Eve version, my mother imitates God, she takes the lead of the Young Ones. There is no Moses? I say. I wasn't able to do it. I had forgotten the names, says my mother. All the same people got out of it OK.

155

May 1st: "We walked in the traces of the past. It's worthless. We went to the Sofitel. It's no longer the Sofitel. It's finished. One mustn't go back to the past."

Monday 22nd: she arrives at noon and says: "I'm old."

Tuesday 23rd: on the telephone she says: "I'm old."

The voice is neutral, guarded. She is on watch.

On Wednesday she is still old. On Thursday I rush to get there happy at the thought of dining with her. She is old. Sitssilent. The meal ends. She gives me several envelopes held together with a paper clip: –Letters for my decease. – But the flowers? I say. – They are fine. We visit the flowers. – Thank you for your visit, she says. She thanks me ten times. I am frightened. This thank you sounds like a farewell. We never say thank you or farewell.

Thursday: "I am *really* old." She observes. Someone rings the doorbell. It's my age knocking at the door. Is it true? She understands something I don't understand. My ears are flayed alive, my heart drowning.

July 1st: Dream of the death of Omi (my grandmother the grandmother) the authorities take me away during the last five days. The authorities do nothing for her. I am desperate. These last solitudes. Hers mine. It is torture. When she is given back to me she is dead. She is lying in the middle of the dream in the cathedral bay in the form of a thick volume. As if exposed in a catafalque. The book, which she now is, is addressed to the dozens of descendants. I want at all costs to come nearer, embrace her, take this book in my arms I moan Omi you whom I love . . .

July 3rd: At midnight thunder falls on the house. The storm bombards. The winds blow their warrior music in all the instruments, in the chimneys, the empty bottles, the hallways howl joyously at death, shake the doors, knock the flowers to the ground. I hear the slight scraping noise of a foot in the rattle-filled sack. I go down quickly. I find my mother standing, in a tale, coming out of the ground with such haste that she didn't have the time to reconstitute herself, she is but a small pink mantle with two immense eyes, above which rise the four white towers from the hair of Cybele, she has nevertheless put on her blue slippers, as if to stay in contact with the familiar ground. Toothless, faceless, flashes of lightning passing in her eyes, she hummurs: – You fell? What is happening? – Not me, I say, the thunder. In her sleep without ears a dull sound reached her that would have raised her from the dead, if she had been in bed. – But I wasn't asleep yet. I thought you had fallen out of bed. She took the thunder for my fall. I am not as deaf as that, she says to me.

She leaves, goes back down, in detail: each step weighed, calculated, measured. By her side, above her, before her, the different persons she has been and is no longer, on her the little pink mantle of truth.

We are extinguished gently, I say to myself, in a sky bathed in light. When I think of all those she has been those German nymphs with heavy ankles and flat stomachs girded with warrior muscles, those travelers who went to taste the countries of the world by the menus, those riders of bicycles and alleys under curfew, those kids full of pranks called Max and Moritz, who deserved to be hanged, geniuses, naïve and powerful divinities of one sex or the other endowed with improbable longevities, without forgetting to mention those charming friends of the beds on which they land and depart with the natural freedom of dragonflies, and the soldiers of the fire, the ones who answer *always* every call for help because they are born for the salvation of mortals,

– I was a midwife, she says
I forgave many stupidities
But there were limits
I had a fat cook

With the beefsteaks deceived me
That one annoyed me
I was a clairvoyant
I was not mean
I was not so very particular
I had quite a few hidden gifts
Without being a daredevil
I didn't know fear
I did things others didn't know how
Against anxiety I was protected
I thought I had a good body
I knew that I was ageless
I was lucky
Luck I don't know if it was luck
I was a midwife
With me everything always went
Gently.

Will the last of the Eves be this lamp of gentleness? She reaches the last step. Standing, at the rail, leaning, as if a ship was moving away from my coast, she looks at me continually until I have disappeared into the depths of the distance.

July 4th: A washed world rises. I alone have crossed the Acheron. The thunder fell before me. My mother arrives smiling, her cheeks pink, during my passage to the other side she has grown still smaller. A hundredth of an inch. Every day. I alone see it. I see the melting. She smiles

Smiling more and more. She wrestles with the angel. Hesitates. Two steps. Enters into the bathroom. I follow her. Hesitates. Thinks. – What did I do? – Hesitates. – At midnight I was not asleep. Thinks – Wrestles. A minute. She smiles. – I am smiling. Finally she finds it again: – I repaired a zipper. Saved. My mother repaired by herself. Repairs me. First thing done after the fall: repair a zipper. She starts up again – life – I become again.

Hesitates. In front of the bathtub. Starts up again. – I am going to take my shower. Thinks. – Wash my hair.

My mother readjusts my disjointed edges. Her hands grow larger.

– You are a magician of resurrection, I say, of metempsychosis.

She clears her throat. Thinks

– Life and death pass so quickly one into the other, I say, that one has a certain anxiety in the morning, it makes me anxious and it reassures me,

in the evening it reassures me and makes me anxious.

– The accounts, I don't want to keep them, she says. They must be li-qui-da-ted

– In September, I say. After the summer. Afterthesummer, I say. This whole story, I say, has an admirable, miraculous side, both because of its unreal, phantasmatic, hallucinatory side, and then naturally, I say, with your magnolian and radiant manner, come from who knows where, of crossing this hallucinatory tempest, it's as if you cured me of my bars

She smiles. – *Kennst du das Wort* Hausirer? No? It's an ambulatory merchant who extols his merchandise from apartment to apartment. You are the somnambulant merchant. You, you extol. Me, I expel. She howls with laughter. At that moment, as if drunk, carried away by the wind of the tale, I heard myself saying, as if after a very very long deliberation secret from myself, before I was able to arrive at a liberation that I have never claimed: "Can you live until one hundred and ten?" I hear the note of insane hope and calculation in the challenge; some force of reality had inspired me the way the gambler hears the voice of chance prompting him what to play. The figure one hundred and ten, *cent dix*, right away took on the mysterious and whispering glow of a mystical sign. I thought I had dreamed it and that it had been revealed to me in secret by someone initiated into the powers of very strong desires, someone from Within, my father perhaps but this was not clear, and what was extraordinary is the sort of incarnation of this number that became a single sign, like the name of a station or a star – moreover I wrote it soon as I heard it as *Sansdis* or *Sansdice*, I felt all the versatilities that were part of its magic, it goes without saying, I was saying to myself, it's a *number*. The word *number* enchanted me in its turn. What a word! I saw myself surrounded by all those noisy fairies in which one doesn't believe, which out of a mistrustful tolerance one confines in the texts of the delirious, all those poets of revelation whom one often forgives for their prophecies especially when they have paid for them at the cost of internments and suicides.

But no matter. I was with the Number. It was clear, precise. From the point of view of figure, it could not displease my mother who is thinking account and bank at this moment. Herself, urged by the umbrage of time, was eager, so as to prepare herself for any extraordinary event, to have all the figures captured and brought under the yoke of her judgment. She spent her days the way a general immersed in the epic unfolding of a large headquarters map projects onto the face of the world all the scenarios of a campaign that is going to change totally the narratives of all the empires,– studying her testament and also like a Talmudist who finds a verse of several lines to incubate – her testament consisting of one page – that gave her *to read* talmudically for hours stretched out – innumerable possibilities of interpretation both purely subjective and private and at the same time with universal consequences, depending on whether she fastened successively on the letter then on the spirit, then first of all on the spirit, then on both, she studied at length the page dated November 2000 and that even as it was written in her hand was no longer in her hand or in her spirit and stood before her from now on like the holy book that would require her to explain herself, to reflect, I saw her reading from bottom to top at length, then she read from top to bottom and that changed everything naturally, later she read mid-page and I saw that then the text was submitted to another Spirit that bothered her, she scratched her forehead, she studied, her lips moved, it is very serious to be in fact the author of several destinies, a word, a figure gets moved, and fortunes for generations are in the balance, it's now that futures are brought into the world, she held the Testament firmly, one guessed the fiery spirit of the beast from the contraction of my mother's hands that were solidly holding the book by both sides, the Testament trembled a little – I saw a swallow cry, pass by, cry, pass by, at her window without her paying it the least attention – she was rereading now from left to right while following with her nose line by line – now here there is something missing she murmured but what – a voice had said to her: I leave the responsibility to you – that irritated her, I saw – after paying inheritance taxes she spelled out and it was not only that but also something else – one thinks of the offense one has to think of who will be offended who will offend who will not be offended who will not offend, to which must be added the forgiveness that will never exist and that sends its unappeasable ghost onto all the battlefields, and my mother was mentally struggling with the figures and discovering with each reading that they had once again changed places and meaning. But she didn't let go, this paper was inexhaustible, it is true, so my mother stood above its face and did not let go her hold, she did not let herself be led around, no, she asked each version *why* it believed it was the most accurate one – there was a truce, she set the paper down on her knees. Sniffed. I had gone out. I returned fifteen minutes later I found her immersed in reading. I worried about her state, I tried some moderate diplomacy, so that she might take a little rest, these talmudixits are as exhausting as the ordeals of shamanism, I say: it seems so to me, I believe. But in vain. The battle began again. Let me think, says my mother. No doubt her spirit was crossing many rivers without golden bough. No one being able to forgive she thought it's in my interest not to make an error.

When I pronounced the Number Sansdice I had the astonished and delightful certainty that I had formed the Golden Number, the Just itself, it appeared to me as obvious, and the absolute, the extremity of the possible that deepens the impossible, I was content, I said to my mother: *Can* you live until one hundred and ten, *cent dix ans*? I pronounced it *disant*, saying. She heard me very well and answered, *without showing the least hesitation*, this: "Yes. Why not? If one can one does. It doesn't bother me if it doesn't bother you."

Thus, everything will always have been up to my will! Right here began for me the New Life. I felt an immense surprise and the happiness of a fresh and blue peace as on the first morning after the overly long anguish. For a few instants I was afraid I would not manage to believe in such admirable news. And naturally I feared seeing my happiness persecuted and poisoned by a swarm of fears and inadvertent acts. Had I indeed said one hundred and ten? Had my mother indeed heard it? She is so deaf. I was enchanted, contented, and suddenly everything crashed? But this fear passed, I believe it was the last one. We had a narrow escape, I thought. I was going to stop us at one hundred. I said to my mother that we had plenty of time for the Testament. But she said to me that she redoes it every ten years or so. I felt happy again. My mother talked to me of magnolias. Two more. I was very active. I took up my work again. I began to write this book, which is to say hers.

TRANSLATOR'S NOTES

Title: *Eve Escapes* might also have been translated as *Eve's Evasion*, which would have captured the repetition in the original title *Ève s'évade*. But "evasion" does not convey the primary sense here of escape, flight, getting away, breaking out, for example from prison. The French title signals that the syllable *ev-* is going to be dispersed significantly across the text in a manner that will evade easy capture in English.

Page 1: *Day of Sufferance* is translating "Jour de souffrance." Among the several possible meanings of the French expression is the sense of a window on sufferance: that is, a window tolerated or permitted by a neighbor. But it also conveys day of suffering and day of delay. See also *pages 24 and 26* for another use in the text.

Page 10: "*Et toi mafille, tu as bien dor-mi?*": "And you my daughter, did you sleep OK?"

Page 29: "It is in a sort of dream that I see her shining before me," etc. Or else "I see it," the tower, which in French takes the same feminine pronoun.

Page 32: "It's a touch of Old Age, a blow from Old Man time!" *C'est un coup de Vieux!* The passage goes on to exploit an amphiboly in this expression, which usually just means "it's a sign of old age."

Page 37: *The Plague*: Albert Camus's 1947 novel, set in Oran, Algeria, during World War II.

Page 38: *La Peau de chagrin*, translated as *The Wild Ass's Skin*: Honoré de Balzac's 1831 novel in which the hero, Raphaël, acquires a magic piece of shagreen that fulfills his desire but each time shrinks a little. Gradually the hero realizes that the length of his life is tied to the size of the magic skin and he attempts to live without desire.

Page 46: "this verse is dead. It is but a worm of dead words without stars." The line plays on the homophones *vers*, verse, and, *ver*, worm.

Also on p. 46: "Tomb tumbling – into ruins," "Tombe – en ruines": "Tombe" here can be read as both the noun meaning "tomb" and the verb "falls," from *tomber*.

Page 65: *"peau de chat"*: cat's skin, but the words echo the title *Peau de chagrin*.

Page 68: *micro*, meaning microphone, echoes the name Mycon.

Page 69: This passage plays on the homophony between *oui* and *ouïe*, the sense of hearing, as well as the sound made by the squirrel.

Page 89: "rise! My mother rises. My Mother-Rises. Lifts," etc. This passage inscribes over and over the mother's name in the ève- syllable: "lève! Ma mère lève. Ma-Mère-Lève. Soulève . . . . enlève, élève, relève: tout. Tout relève d'Ève . . ."

Page 102: "A new arising": again the phrase inscribes the name Ève in a significant way: in "Un nouveau lever" one can also hear a phrase that would mean "A new Eve is."

Page 119: To do something *d'arrache-pied* is to do it relentlessly or without stopping, but literally the phrase means tearing off a foot.

Page 129: "The conductor's not a doctor." The rhyme in the original makes more sense of this exchange: *"Le conducteur, c'est pas l'heure."* "Pas l'heure," "not time," sounds like "pâleur," "paleness," hence the question "How do you spell it?"

Page 131: "we have arrived at The Eve," that is, "La Veille," the day or night before. But *veille* also means the watch or the wake.

Page 133: *D'or/dort*: golden and sleeps.

Page 134: *honi soit qui y pense*, or "shame to whoever thinks of it," is a revision of the ancient motto *honi soit qui mal y pense*, shame to whoever thinks ill of it.

mord: from *mordre*, to bite, but also a homophone of *mort*, death

Page 136: BHV is the Bazar de l'Hôtel de Ville, a large department store in the center of Paris.

Also on p. 136: Damart is the name of a catalogue retailer of clothing.

Page 152: *qui naît*, who or which is born, *qui n'est*, who or which is not.

Page 160: "*Sansdis* or *Sansdice*": homophones of the two possible pronunciations of the number *cent dix*.